Not Exactly
What I
Had in Mind

Not Exactly What I Had in Mind

An Incurable Love Story

ROSEMARY BRESLIN

VILLARD BOOKS / RANDOM HOUSE

VILLARD BOOKS is a registered trademark of Random House, Inc.

Library of Congress Cataloging-in-Publication Data

Breslin, Rosemary.
Not exactly what I had in mind / Rosemary Breslin.
p.   cm.
ISBN: 0-812-99228-8
1. Breslin, Rosemary.   2. Patients—United States—Biography.
3. Women—United States—Biography.   I. Title.
CT275.B656A3   1997
974.7'1043—dc21
[B]   96-49639

Random House website address: http://www.randomhouse.com
Printed in the United States of America on acid-free paper

For
my family
and
Giorgio Armani

Not Exactly
What I
Had in Mind

The Present

I think I found my husband's next wife. Since we bought this tiny cottage in the country a few months back I'd been in search of a good breakfast place that opens early. Much as I love diners and beat-up coffee shops, the coffee never has a good kick and the muffins almost always have the consistency of paperweights. I found a great one that serves thick, strong coffee and light, fresh muffins. As I stood on line to order, I immediately turned my eye to the women who run the place. Standing together, they were good-looking, hardworking, hip. They could handle things.

Of the two, Ann's the one I chose on the spot. I first saw her at the grill, in the early morning rush of farmers and truckers and laborers and newcomers like me, second-home owners from the big city, and she was great to watch. Thin, muscular, hair loosely pulled back, up before four but still looking great as she fills the orders with great efficiency, cutting off slabs of fresh cinnamon bread or flipping orders of thick hash browns.

Ann and I hit it off immediately. We started out the usual way. A smile. A nod of recognition. A wave good-bye after I paid for my papers and order. Then we got to talking. I told her I'd just bought my house and she told me she had been a biochemist in Washington, D.C., who had been lured back to her hometown by her sister, who had taken over a convenience store and turned it into this breakfast place.

Soon I started bringing Tony, my husband, Ann's future husband, with me. He didn't come along at first because I get up so much earlier, but I lured him out the door with the image of frying bacon and pancakes so large and light that when they're placed in front of you, you feel as if you're a kid in a fairy tale.

Ann already dug me by the time I introduced her to Tony. We'd been checking each other out and romancing each other the way women do, so when Ann saw the way I feel about Tony, he was right in there. Then the other morning, as Tony and I were leaving, Ann said that once in a while she and her sister throw dinner parties at night after they close and she took our number to call us. It was nice because we don't know anybody yet, unless you count the Terminix guy. But it was long before the dinner invitation that I had chosen Ann for Tony, although I hadn't mentioned it to him until we were on our way home last Sunday morning.

"You could marry her," I said, as I shut the Jeep door. "She'd be good for you."

Tony tried to pretend he didn't know what I was talking about, but since we've had this conversation on a couple of occasions he caught on pretty quickly.

"Will you shut up," he responded.

"I'm serious. I can see her." What I meant was he'd be OK with her, she'd understand him, appreciate both him and the love and work I'd put into him. Tony was a good guy when I met him, but I made him great. So I'm not giving him up to just any old tramp.

"You're not going anywhere," Tony said.

"That's what you say."

"That's what I have to say," Tony said.

And I guess he does. What good is it going to do him to worry that this illness I have may kill me sooner rather than later. I like to think the same way he does, but sometimes I worry. Even with some major rough spots, I have managed to stay alive with this serious blood disease for six years now. Still, a rare and serious disorder like mine is not exactly a ringing endorsement for longevity. Tony has to say nothing's going to happen to me, and I have to be prepared for the possibility. I guess that's what they call balance.

Essentially this illness affects my red blood cells. Doctors speculate that perhaps I caught a virus or had a toxic reaction and that my body created an antibody to fight the invader. Doctors believe the antibody successfully fought the virus or toxic reaction, but did not stop there. It apparently can't differentiate between the now defeated invader and my healthy red blood cells. The antibody attacks the cells just before they are released from the bone marrow. As a result, my body is unable to produce mature red blood cells. Doctors have made up a lot of fancy names for this illness, but when you get right down to it it's anemia. Just not the kind you take iron pills for. It is truly because of the miracles of modern science that I am alive.

Almost all the doctors familiar with my case have speculated that this illness may disappear as mysteriously as it first appeared, though as the years pass I believe this less and less. Especially since it's now going stronger than ever. No one

knows the cause of this disorder or how to cure it, and to
figure out a way to treat it has been "a crapshoot," to quote
one of the country's foremost hematologists. In case my illness
doesn't seem special enough, no one has seen it before. At
least none of the many doctors I have seen or contacted
around the world.

So my story isn't a simple one. Not quite Ali MacGraw in
Love Story. Well, maybe the Tony part of my story. I'd
already been sick for two years when I met Tony. We've been
together for four years, married for three. I hope it'll be thirty-
three someday, but that seems unlikely. If I boast a little about
what I've done for Tony, it doesn't compare with what he's
done for me. He's my whole life.

I may hate being sick, I do want it to go away desperately,
but I can no longer wish it never happened, because all the
horrors I've endured for these past six years are a great part of
the woman I've become. I don't know who I would be if this
hadn't happened to me. And the woman I've become is the
woman who fell in love with Tony Dunne, and I couldn't give
that up for anything in the entire world. Not even in exchange
for my life. So yes, imagining Tony marrying Ann is a little
bit of a joke. But just a little.

The Meeting

I guess the thing I remember most about the night we met was that I smelled. It's not something you easily forget. If you want to get technical, I didn't smell but my gray cashmere pullover did. I first noticed it as I reached for the wine carafe on the table with my right arm, which meant I leaned right in front of Tony, and I got a little whiff of my own body odor. For the rest of the evening I kept my arms pinned to my sides. The fact that I wore a smelly sweater says a lot about where I was at that time. To say my life had bottomed out would be a good beginning.

At this point I had let my illness rob me of just about everything, including my apartment. On this night, the night we met, I was already packing boxes so I could move into a cordoned-off section of my younger cousin's living room. Just where you want your life to be at thirty-three.

On this Thursday night, friends had asked me to the theater and dinner, and I said yes because I was too embarrassed to say I couldn't afford it. Forget the theater and dinner part,

I couldn't afford the cab to get there. And I couldn't afford to dry-clean my sweater, although if I'd had any motivation at all I would have handwashed it. But I didn't care. The most I did to get ready was to take my hair out of a ponytail.

Six of us went to see John Leguizamo in his one-man show *Mambo Mouth* and then to Orso's for dinner. A real Manhattan evening. I had managed to scrounge together a few bucks, money meant for the telephone bill.

I had no idea I was being set up, but apparently everyone else knew. Several of our mutual friends had tried for over a year to get Tony and me to meet, but it hadn't worked out. If anyone had told me about this, I would never have come.

Tony was aware this whole evening was designed for us to meet, and until this day he believes I'm being dishonestly naive when I say I wasn't, but I'm not. A woman who wears a smelly sweater to dinner definitely does not know she's being set up. I'm certain Amy Vanderbilt will back me up on this one.

At the round dinner table, Tony sat to my right. We fell into easy conversation, but I gave it no real thought. I do remember that a few times the conversation with the others got a little jaded-Manhattan. In particular, one friend's date started talking about her favorite city, and of course I had to chime in that while I agreed with her that Paris is Paris, I much preferred Hong Kong. Everybody's got his or her asshole side, and mine comes out when I have the need to prove I'm somebody, which is probably when it happens to most people. Tony, of course, was silent when the conversation took turns such as this. Fortunately, there were only a few of those during the evening, so I only felt like sort of a jerk on my way home. I really don't remember what I talked to Tony about and usually I have great recall, but I remember ending the night thinking he was a great guy and I really liked him. And, oh, how I hoped he wouldn't call me. Though this may sound disingenuous, with all my heart I didn't want him to call because I had nothing to offer. Not to myself, nor anybody else.

And that feeling wasn't wholly connected to being sick. I'd shut off about men a long time before. I hadn't been on a date for over three and a half years, quite a long time before I'd gotten sick. I was never much for dating and had never been in a good relationship. As screwed up as my life might be, both before and after I got sick, there was nothing in it that a guy wouldn't make worse. So when I say I didn't want Tony to call, I meant it.

The group of us had gone out on Thursday night. Tony called the following Monday. My friend Bram later told me Tony had called him first thing on Friday for my number.

"So why'd he wait till Monday," I asked.

"No guy's gonna call you the first time on a Friday or Saturday. He'd never want you to think he had nothing to do." Oh, and it's women who play the games.

Tony called on Monday and asked me out for the next night. I'd never felt so comfortable about anyone before, so easy. But maybe it was also because I knew it couldn't go anywhere. That's all there was to it.

Still, I changed my clothes at least four times for the date. This is not an exaggeration, and if I were at all introspective, maybe it would have meant something to me at the time. In the end I went with a white shirt, jeans and a blue blazer. We met at Gallagher's, a steak house in the West Fifties. I hadn't been there since I was a kid when my father worked at the nearby *Herald Tribune* and my mother would take us there to meet him. It always seemed as if we sat there for hours, and

I'm sure we did. I remember the waiters would give my two brothers and me steak tips and bread sticks, and every half hour or so my father would call and tell my mother, "Fifteen more minutes." I'd say that's the story of his life when he's on deadline. Fifteen more minutes. In those precomputer days when they set the newspaper type by hand, editors used to have to physically take his stories away from him. Pull the pages out of the typewriter and give them to the typesetters. And while he wrote we would wait at the restaurant. Major sports figures used to come into the restaurant in those days and that always excited my brothers. Me, I was just happy with the steak in front of me and knocking back a few Shirley Temples. Born weighing ten pounds six ounces, clearly I have had a healthy appetite since before birth and it hasn't failed me since.

Of course, on my first real date with Tony I played the girl game and did not eat like the truck driver I truly am. And worse, since food is one of the few things I take seriously, the waiter gave Tony my steak. I ordered mine rare and he ordered his medium rare. One knife-cut into mine and I saw it was too done. A glance over at Tony's steak, which he was digging into in large bites, and I saw it was done to perfection. He was oblivious to the fact that he was eating my dinner, and I must have already really liked him because I kept my mouth shut and didn't grab the plate away from him as I wanted to. In the end, since mine tasted a little like dry cardboard, it helped me eat a civilized amount.

The one thing my friend Bram had told me about Tony was that he'd been married for about eight months in his early twenties and it had affected him deeply. Tony was now in his mid thirties. I try to be sensitive, but when Tony mentioned his marriage I sat there thinking to myself, This is a little odd, get past it already. But then he said something that caught my attention. After I got home that evening I called Bram and said, "Eight years, not eight months. Just a slight difference."

As on the first night I can hardly remember what else Tony and I talked about. I do remember that I alluded to this "slight blood problem I'd had." Notice the past tense.

We parted on the corner of Fifty-second and Seventh Avenue, lingering with more to talk about, as there almost always is in those early stages of discovery. I can picture Tony so perfectly in his blue blazer, so easy to see the little boy in his sweet face. And when I think back on it now it always makes me warm inside, and I guess that though I hardly knew him, I recognized how hard he was trying. Although it would be two more dates before I realized I was in love with him, I know now that I already loved him as we stood on that street corner. But that does not mean I wanted to see him again. I had never known this feeling, and it made me want him to go away even more. I was having a good time playing at normal life, but it was a fantasy and it was going to end. And anyway, I really did not have the cab fare for another date.

Still, as I walked up Third Avenue the next morning with my friend Abigail, she asked, "Is it too early to talk about marriage?"

"No," I answered.

I was going to milk this fantasy for all it was worth. I could play at dating and marriage and revel in it for a few days, and then when it ended I could carry the gentle memory with me. I figured we could be friends, and maybe I could interest him in one of my many available girlfriends.

On our second date we went to see a terrible movie with Matt Dillon and Sean Young. I paid for the tickets, aware that now both the phone and electricity were soon to be shut off.

On the third date we went to see *La Femme Nikita,* and

living recklessly, I again paid for the tickets. Afterward, we ate dinner at a little Italian restaurant. Until now, I had deftly avoided Tony's asking me too much about myself by always asking him a lot of questions. But on that night, I decided it was at the point where my omission was going to seem like a lie, which it was. "I think there's a few things I should tell you," I said as he forked a plate of spaghetti with baby clams. "You know that little blood problem I mentioned I'd had. Well, it's not exactly little and it's not exactly in the past." We were about halfway through the meal, and you might say this got his attention.

The Beginning

It all started with a headache. It was the winter of 1989, and I got this headache in the front of my head that wouldn't go away. Of course, I never considered going to a doctor because that would have made sense. Instead, I took a lot of aspirin, which didn't do anything, and assumed I had a brain tumor. As the winter wore on, I either got used to the throbbing in my brain or it went away, but by then the headache was the least of my problems. I don't know if it was the shortness of breath or the night sweats that I noticed first, but by then I knew it was not a brain tumor. I knew I had AIDS and I knew who gave it to me. A little over a year before, a long relationship with a guy who had cheated on me with every woman who walked into his restaurant had ended. This was a guy who took me to Paris and picked out lingerie for another woman, saying it was for his sister. As if I bought that. But still, I stuck around. The worst part of the whole thing was that we had had infrequent and terrible sex. I mean the worst. So bad that I knew none was better. And now I was going to die because of it, and I'd never even had an orgasm with him. I'm not big on feeling sorry for myself, but it sure seems if you're going to end up dead, the sex should be very, very good.

I didn't tell anyone what I suspected, and for several months I was able to hide how sick I felt. Still, each night, I had to switch from one side of the bed to the other because the sheets were soaked. By this time a smarter person would have gone to a doctor, but as I was fading fast and furiously, I saw no need. And anyway, I knew what was wrong with me, and I only hoped the creep went first.

There was a bright side. For the very first time in my life I had no appetite. The only thing I really ate was Stoned Wheat Thins and a few Cokes. I was like, hey, I could get used to this. The other thing was on the few occasions I had enough strength to go out, all my friends commented on my beautiful skin. It was like porcelain, pale and perfect. I finally looked the way I had dreamed about for my whole life, and now I was going to die.

But then it did get to the point where all my friends started to notice something was wrong, so I lied and said I'd gone to the doctor and I was a little anemic. That sounded good. And I still managed to work. I was working on a rewrite of a script for a producer who had bought the script in the first place because he liked the title. The fact that the original script was unreadable didn't seem to be a problem. The producer asked me to develop the story into a sexual farce about a rogue chauffeur who was to be played by Mikhail Baryshnikov. I saw Baryshnikov on Broadway, where everyone was raving about his work in the play *The Metamorphosis*, the one where the guy turns into a bug. I saw the show three times, and each time I was more astounded by Misha's agility. He was an incredible contortionist, but I could not understand a single line of his dialogue. Maybe we should make him a dancing chauffeur, I thought. Still, I was getting paid, and there's quite a bit to be said for that.

So the project wore on and so did my self-diagnosed illness, which brought me from the bed to my desk to the couch and back into my bed at night. In the span of a few short weeks it became impossible for me to leave the house. By then, a new condition had set in. I started to get incredibly painful cramping in my hands, and they would get locked in claw-like positions for a few seconds at a time. I was certain the end was near and hoped it would happen before I had to make my next rent payment.

Then, on a rainy, cold Thursday evening my friend Patricia asked me to meet her and her son for dinner at a hamburger joint. Though it was only six blocks from my house, once I got to the corner I had to rest against the side of the bus shelter, and I realized I could never walk it and ended up taking the bus.

I made my way to their table in the back of the restaurant. By this time, sitting up was getting hard and halfway through the meal I said I had to go home, just as a couple arrived at the table next to ours. I made it to the front of the restaurant, right by the cash register, and then the entire floor started to move and I had to lean against the wall. I don't know what I looked like, but it must have been pretty bad because the manager rushed over to help me. "I just need some air," I said and he helped me outside, where I sat on the stoop of a brownstone in the cold early-April drizzle. The manager rushed back in to get Patricia, and I'd like to think he was being helpful, but even in my hazy condition I got the distinct impression that he thought I was bad for business. He was right. As Patricia rose from the table the couple who had passed me on my way out stopped her and asked, "Was it something she ate?"

Outside, with the rain sliding down my face, I told Patricia I really was fine, I just hadn't been feeling well and needed to go home. She hailed a cab, and as she helped me in the driver turned and asked, "She isn't going to throw up, is she?"

"No, she's fine," Patricia said and pushed me inside. On the ride home, she made me swear I would see a doctor the next day and I said yes. I had no intention of going because I knew I had so few days left so why bother.

But I did go to the doctor the next day because early that morning my father called. When Patricia had gotten home that night, her Mom-antennae at full power, she decided she didn't trust me. She called my father: "Something's really wrong with Rosemary. She has to go to the doctor."

So here he was pounding on my door the next morning with my sister, Kelly, in tow. As they sat at my dining room table and immediately started fighting about money, it was only to shut them up that made me say, "Would you please stop. I don't feel well." Anything not to listen to the dialogue the two of them had had for over a decade. When I called my family doctor, his assistant told me to come right over because the doctor was leaving for the weekend in a few hours.

The easiest thing would have been for my father to go with me, but he didn't want to because he had bad memories of the office, since it was where my mother had been treated before she died of cancer nine years before. So he dropped me off there and arranged for my stepmother to meet me. I don't know where my sister got lost in the shuffle, but I was a little worried about her being left alone in my apartment because she always viewed that as a prime opportunity to lift a few clothes, make a few long-distance phone calls, forge a couple of checks and charge a few things on credit cards. My sister thinks the Home Shopping Network is my house.

So as I sat in the doctor's waiting room and wondered what pieces of jewelry would be missing I decided that I didn't have AIDS, it was probably flu or something else, and that the doctor would see me, prescribe a few pills and send me on my way. Self-delusion can be a beautiful thing.

Instead, when the doctor came to greet me he looked at me and said nothing except "We have a problem." He ushered me into the examining room and said he'd never seen anyone quite so pale. As he held the stethoscope to my chest, he asked, "Haven't you noticed your heart's been racing? Haven't you been having trouble breathing?" Those would be the least of my problems, I wanted to say, but instead shrugged sheepishly and answered, "I figured I had some kind of flu that would go away."

After a quick examination he told me he was sending me to a hematologist. At the time, I'm not sure I even knew what one was. My stepmother and I took a cab uptown, where my father was now going to meet us; this office held no bad memories for him because he had never been there. Some of my own memories about that morning are a little vague, but I remember one nurse taking a lot of blood from my arm and then the hematologist telling me I was going to have a bone marrow test. As I lay facedown on the examining table, I was wondering what happened to giving me a little prescription and a little bed rest. I also figured by now my sister was having a tag sale back at my apartment.

I must have been incredibly scared because I don't remember the bone marrow exam's hurting very much, even though the hematologist also took a sliver of bone from my right hip.

What I remember quite clearly is sitting in the doctor's office afterward, waiting for him to tell me what I needed to do and then send me on my way. He asked me a few questions about how I was feeling and how long this had been going on. I told him I had started feeling sluggish about six weeks before, but that it had gotten steadily worse over the last three weeks. During our conversation a lab technician walked in with a printout as the doctor asked, "Why didn't you see someone sooner?"

Quietly I confessed, "I thought I had AIDS, so I figured there was no point."

He didn't seem surprised by my response. "I'll give you a test, but from what I can see you're exhibiting the exact opposite symptoms of someone with AIDS." He paused. "And I think we can rule out leukemia, although we'll need to run some more tests."

Leukemia? I thought. How'd he come up with that one? Needless to say, I was not deriving much comfort from the direction this conversation was taking.

"So what do I do now?" I asked.

"You have to go to the hospital," he answered.

"I can't go to the hospital."

"You have to. You're going to need a few pints of blood. Right now, you're very anemic."

"What's wrong with me?"

"We don't know yet. But we have to find out. We're arranging for a room now."

I'm screwed, I thought, but asked, "Isn't there some other way?"

I probably should have been worrying about dying, but what was foremost in my mind was health insurance. I was pretty sure I didn't have any. At the hematologist's office I'd given my old Blue Cross number from when I had worked at a newspaper. Since I'd been writing movie scripts for the last year, I had had to join the Writers Guild, and the insurance paperwork had been sitting on my desk for many months. I'd never even had a cold, so I had figured someday I'd get around to it. And I had figured it probably would cost me some money, and since I was spending it a little more quickly than I made it, I had put health insurance well behind a new pair of Robert Clegerie loafers. My attitude about health insurance was why pay for something you never use. So now I was screwed because of my stupidity. Not a new situation for me.

At the waiting room for admission to the hospital, I took a seat and waited. I didn't ask my father how he felt about being here, as this was where my mother had died. And I felt really awful that my father thought my not wanting to go to the hospital was connected to my mother when really it was all about money. I figured I'd get him alone later and tell him about my little dilemma. He'd understand. I do remember as I slumped in my seat waiting I heard the buzz around the room that Jimmy Breslin was there. My father is a newspaper columnist and author and extremely recognizable in New York City, where we live.

Now, to be accommodating, one of the admissions volunteers tells my father they'll try to get me a room quickly, but adds, "There's no private rooms right now, but maybe we can move her later." All this movement is more activity than I've had in six weeks and I can hardly sit up. I hear the word "private" and a knife goes through my heart. How the hell am I going to pay for that? "I don't want a private room," I say to both the woman and my father. "It's not necessary." My father gives me a look that says he's impressed I don't expect special treatment. And I'm thinking maybe they've got a room with a group rate. When I fill out the admissions form I again write down my expired insurance number, figuring by the time they catch up to me I'll either be dead or have figured a way out of this mess. I think I could probably hock a few items if my sister hasn't already wiped me out.

After that, I was taken into a little room, hooked up to an EKG machine, then whisked off to another floor to get a chest X ray, and somewhere along the way someone stuck a needle in my arm and took more blood. It seemed everybody wanted some of the one thing I didn't have. The scenario that followed is the one hospital routine I will never get used to. They have an attendant take you to wait all by yourself in hallways and rooms at a time when you are at your most vulnerable. I have never understood why one person from your family or a friend can't come with you. As much as all my visits to hospitals have a haziness to them, the times I have been taken off alone have always remained crystal clear. And when you're sitting alone in a wheelchair—thirty-two years old and never having had a cold in your life—in the hospital where your mother died and where you suspect you might die, that is when you could really use someone with you.

Finally, I was deposited in a room with an elderly woman whose family owned a funeral parlor in Astoria, Queens. I was given the bed by the window, and now, late on a Friday afternoon, several of my five siblings had arrived. My sister, surely busy with her size 8 sample sale, didn't arrive until the next day.

A few minutes after I settled in, a lab technician appeared with a big basket on her arm. She reminded me of something out of "Little Red Riding Hood," but the goodies filling her basket were glass vials. The technician pulled out a tourniquet and I said quietly, "I think they just did that downstairs."

"That's impossible," she announced.

I pointed to the Band-Aid on my inner arm and said, "They took a lot of vials just a little while ago."

"It must have been for something else."

Still, she got up and left the room. When she returned she announced there was no record of it on the computer, so it must not have happened. So, ready to acquiesce but sure that it did happen and with a Band-Aid to prove it, I meekly offered, "Well, maybe it was for something else."

"There's nothing on the computer," she again responded and again left the room. About an hour or so later she returned and said the missing vials had been located. They were needed to type and cross my blood, which is what is done prior to giving someone a blood transfusion. And so I learned in the first hours of my first hospital experience to stay on top of everything. It's amazing the number of things that can go wrong, and I often wonder how someone truly out of it survives a hospital stay.

A resident now stuck an intravenous needle in my arm and hooked me up to the first unit of blood. It turned out I was O positive. Although I should have been wondering about the larger question of what was happening to me, I was wondering about the more immediate one, "What does a bag of blood cost?" I had figured the hospital room was about three hundred dollars and I decided a bag of blood couldn't cost more than one thousand dollars. Now the question was how many of these I could afford. I finally decided to get my father alone later and discuss my little dilemma. He'd be a little unhappy, but what choice did I really have. In the meantime, the woman beside me had taken to moaning.

A parade of family members passed through my room and I was getting a little edgy, as I was now on bag number three. "How many of these do you think I'm going to need?" I asked the resident in a very small voice. "We're not sure," he replied. "Your red blood count is very, very low. We'll test you after every two or three units until we get you up to a normal range." I thought to myself, You're such a screwup. You should be here giving all your energy to getting better, and all you can worry about is the money because you didn't mail back the insurance forms thinking you'd have to send money and you spent the money on clothes that your sister is now selling or stealing. I knew I had to get my father alone.

And finally, later in the evening, I did. He sat beside my bed and started ruminating. "This is the kind of thing that breaks families," he said. "If this were your sister, we'd be ruined. I've been screaming at her about health insurance, but she doesn't follow through. I told her I'd pay for the insurance, but she stood the guy up for the mandatory blood test. Something like this destroys lives."

Why couldn't I die peacefully at home, I thought. What did I do to deserve this? I just mutely nodded my head as my father continued talking and thought, I am really fucked.

When my brother Kevin arrived a few minutes later, we finally convinced my father he should go home and rest, that I was fine and was going to sleep soon and Kevin would stay with me for a little while. My father thought it was so nice that my relationship with my older brother is so close, which it is, and that I wanted to be alone with him. I managed to contain myself for one beat after my father left before I confided in Kevin.

"I've got a big problem," I said and started to cry.

"It's going to be all right," he answered, not too convincingly.

"Not this," I said. "I don't have any health insurance."

"What do you mean?" he said.

"I had the forms and I meant to send them in but I didn't.

I've got a few thousand dollars in the bank and a check coming, but all over this hospital are signs that you can't be released until your bill is settled, and I gave an expired insurance number which I'm sure they're going to catch on to."

"I'll go down to the billing office tomorrow and see what I can work out," he answered, and though it made me feel a tiny bit better it didn't help much, and when they brought the next bag of blood I wondered if there was a bulk discount rate.

And so, on my first night in the hospital since my birth, I worried about money and dying and listened to the moans of the woman on the other side of the curtain while a bag of blood hovered over me and dripped slowly into my vein. I didn't think things could get much worse until in the middle of the night the moaning woman started talking to me. "Can you help me?" she wailed. "Can you help me?"

"I don't know," I said.

"I went to the bathroom in the bed. I tried to ring for the nurse to tell her I had to get up, but nobody came and now I've got shit all over myself." Fortunately, a nurse came a few moments later, and there was a lot of moving about on the other side of the curtain. I looked out the window into the now dark night and thought I must be a very, very bad person if this was happening to me.

The next day passed in a haze, with doctors stopping by to talk to me, and the bags of blood being delivered and left to drip slowly into my left arm. I was starting to give in to how exhausted I really was and spent the Saturday afternoon dozing on and off. In the background, on the other side of the curtain, the sounds of a baseball game filled the room and finally so penetrated my brain that I woke in a panic. That baseball game. It's been going on forever. I thought I was losing my mind and the way it was manifesting itself was in a never-ending baseball game. "Relax," my brother Kevin said. "It's a doubleheader. It's been on all afternoon." My room-mate's husband was also there, and for five or six hours that afternoon he watched the game and never spoke. By the afternoon, the resident stopped by and told me they would let me out the next morning, Sunday. I needed a few more units of blood, and then they would watch me overnight. That would make it seven units of blood in all, which, at the time, didn't mean much to me. I was a little more relaxed about the money thing because my brother Kevin was armed with every credit card he had and was headed down to see the cashier. When Kevin returned he told me the guy in billing wouldn't let him pay, it would cause too much confusion. He believed if I was an active union member I did have insurance, and that I could find out everything on Monday and then call the hospital. As this was Saturday and I was being released on Sunday, I thought I could make a clean escape, but I was not going to take any chances. Saturday night was a repeat of the night before with my roommate and by 6 A.M., still with the IV stuck in my arm I was up and dressed and sitting in a chair. The last bag of blood had finished sometime during the night, and now I had some saline dripping in. Around seven the resident came in and ordered a blood test and said I could be released after the results. On guard, I had a plan in place. I called Kevin, woke him up and said, "Come get me." Then I called my father and lied. "They haven't told me when I'm going to be released, so don't rush over."

"I'm going to come now."

"No, no, wait. I'll call you after the doctor comes."

As each minute ticked, I got more nervous. I envisioned my father arriving just as a nurse was blocking my path saying I couldn't go anywhere, that I owed the hospital ten thousand dollars and I'd better pay up. Ten thousand dollars was the figure I had arrived at after much revision during the last two days.

With the IV in my arm I wriggled out of the hospital gown and back into the blue jeans and black-and-white pony shirt I had worn to the hospital. I remember everything about that outfit—the jeans were Italian and baggy and the shirt was from Paul Smith. When I took that outfit off that day, I could never bring myself to put it on again and finally put it in the incinerator room. I couldn't even give it to charity because maybe it would bring someone bad karma. And it was too bad, because I dug the jeans.

Finally, a nurse arrived with some discharge papers, and I held out my arm with the sleeve rolled up and she removed the IV. At the same time, I signed the papers, handed them to her and waited for her to tell me I wasn't going anywhere. But she said nothing.

"Is that it?" I asked quietly.

"Is someone coming for you?"

I nodded.

"Then you can go." On cue, Kevin arrived. I called my father. "Kevin came by and they just said I can leave. So he'll drop me off."

For once, things were going slightly my way. As we walked down the hall to the elevator I picked up my pace. Probably prisoners getting released do the same thing, sure they're going to stop and drag you back. But nobody did.

And so we hailed a cab on Lexington Avenue and Kevin dropped me off. At my father and stepmother's. During my hospital stay, the doctors had decided I was too sick to stay home alone. At thirty-two, moving in with Stepmom and Dad. Life is just full of fun surprises.

Am I Gilda Radner?

First things first. By early Monday afternoon my brother Kevin had spoken with someone from my union, who informed him, "Of course she's covered. We were just waiting for her to fill out the information form and beneficiary form. But she's been covered since last summer." The absolutely unnecessary anguish I'd put myself through over the whole insurance thing is so typical of me. I always put off a simple thing like filling out a piece of paper and then wait until in my own mind it becomes completely overwhelming. For four years I didn't file taxes, and it finally got to the point I couldn't sleep at night and then I was sure I owed them so much money I could never pay. Then I was embarrassed to go to an accountant with this problem, but I finally did, and for most of those back years I was owed money. In total I owed the IRS a little over four thousand dollars, not an insignificant sum, but not worth all the breakdowns I'd had in the middle of the night. You'd think I'd learn from these things, but I don't. I just keep on doing them.

So here I was, ensconced in my father's house, relieved of the pressure that I wasn't going to destroy my family financially, and finally free to ponder how sick I really was. My body was so worn-out I hardly had enough energy to leave the house, except to walk across the street to Central Park to sit on a bench. Even this exhausted me. At night I still had incredible sweats that soaked the sheets. I was in a room with twin beds so I would just switch. I wondered a lot about what was happening to me, but mostly I sat around too sick to do much of anything.

And then there were visits to doctors, doctors in all shapes and sizes. Early on, several theories involved my spleen. Every doctor I saw poked around my left side and shook his head negatively. It didn't seem enlarged, they'd say. Finally, the hematologist, for about the tenth time, started probing it and asked if it hurt. "Yes, it does," I said and burst into tears. He sent me for a CAT (computerized axial tomography) scan, where they would inject me with radioactive iodine and then place me, on a stretcher, inside a machine that takes pictures of my insides. Basically, a fancy X ray. The hematologist called the Upper East Side office of the doctors who own and operate this expensive machine. My father took me over there.

When we arrived, a tall patrician doctor met us in the waiting room. I should say he met Jimmy Breslin. The doctor glanced my way once, but only because I happened to be standing there looking pale and pathetic. Otherwise, he would have ignored me completely. Doctors, as a group, love celebrities more than any other people I have ever met. While the doctor chatted with my father, I was asked to fill out forms and pay. Feeling flush now that I knew I had excellent insurance, I found this office accepted only checks or credit cards as payment for the use of the machine. In my case $450. On this day I had to borrow the money from my father. I would have been turned away if I hadn't come up with the bucks.

I was then led to a little closet, where I changed, and into a room, where I lay on a stretcher. The doctor then made a cameo appearance, carefully checked my arm for a vein, since every doctor and nurse so far had cautioned me that I had poor ones. He then hooked me up to intravenous iodine that would illuminate my abdomen for the machine. A technician in a windowed room gave me instructions through a speaker, but I couldn't make out the muffled words. She angrily came out and said, "When I say 'Breathe,' do that. When I say 'Don't breathe,' don't."

Forget that I was alone and crying on a table, and she hadn't given me any instructions in advance or even what she would be saying over the speaker. I was wasting precious time. The machine is money.

After taking pictures of my insides for maybe five minutes, it was all over. I got out of there as quickly as possible, disliking the place intensely.

The next day my spleen was pronounced fine. It turned out that my side was bruised from so many doctors' poking it.

Another doctor had a theory that my thymus gland was my problem. Still trying to figure out what was wrong with me, my hematologist sent me back for another CAT scan for a head and chest scan; the thymus—I have no idea what it is— is located near the throat. This time the hematologist's secretary called the other CAT scan doctors' office and spoke with a secretary there. When my father and I arrived, no doctor came out and bowed to Jimmy Breslin. They weren't expecting him.

Again, I lay on the stretcher. A different doctor, the partner, came rushing into the room, clearly in a hurry. As he grabbed the needle attached to the IV, I said meekly, "I've got bad veins. Everyone has trouble finding a good one."

"I see plenty of good ones," he answered brusquely and plunged the needle into my left arm. Nothing. He took the needle out. The technician handed him a new one, and the doctor plunged in again while she wrapped gauze on the blood dripping from his first attempt. His second try failed. So did his third and fourth. By this time he had switched to my right arm. He took no time in between, just kept plunging different needles into my arms. As little rivulets of blood dripped down my arms, the technician visibly winced at what the doctor was doing to me.

On the fifth try, the doctor again stuck the needle in on the inside of my left elbow. "What was that?" I cried out, feeling a tugging in my arm and a hot flash in the palm of my hand. The doctor said nothing and just plunged another needle in, this time finally finding a good vein. He then raced from the room. The whole thing took maybe two minutes.

After the CAT scan was over, I ran through the waiting room and out onto the sidewalk. I took off my jacket and exposed my arms with six gauze bandages on them. "Look at what he did to me," I said to my father, partly in anger but mostly in disbelief. My father, feeling helpless, wanted to go back inside, but I wouldn't let him. There is a down side to most things, and in this case if he went back in he wouldn't be an irate father whose daughter had been mistreated, he would be Jimmy Breslin, expecting preferential treatment and throwing a tantrum. I said, "Let's just get out of here."

When I got home that night I called a friend who has great medical expertise. Peter had never heard of someone trying for a vein more than three times. If a vein can't be found on the first or second attempt, a decent person puts a hot cloth on

the area or soaks it in hot water or spends a long time search-
ing before trying again. This doctor had not done any of these
things. Peter also told me that what had happened on that
fifth attempt was that the doctor had hit a nerve. Yet he had
said not a word. It would be well over a year before the
tugging in my arm went away. This was really my first and
only example of a truly bad doctor, someone whose behavior I
consider almost criminal. I've never forgotten him, and for a
long time afterward he played a major role in a revenge fantasy of mine.

Doctors had a final theory that this anemia might be a freak
thing and would simply go away. But as the weeks wore on,
my red blood cell count, the indicator of what was going on,
began to drop again. This was not simply going away. I had
several blood transfusions of a few pints at the hematologist's
office, but the cell count still continued to drop. Finally, I
needed too large a transfusion to get it at the doctor's office
and was informed I'd have to spend one night in the hospital.

At the hospital admissions the volunteer informed us there
was only one room available. I was placed in a room with a
woman who was maybe my age, but so ravaged by cancer it
was hard to tell. Her mother was assembling her belongings
and chatting cheerfully about their going home that afternoon.
A nurse then entered and told me my new roommate was
being wheeled around the hospital on a stretcher getting various tests and would be arriving in a few hours. "She's eighty-
four and very sick," the nurse said.

"I want a private room" was my response. Now I could be
a big shot. I was a paying customer, and I was ready to cash
in big-time on my father's celebrity. I didn't care. Call me
callous, but I just wasn't up for another incontinent old lady. I
had my own problems.

My aunt, my mother's sister, was in the room with me when the nurse said a private room was available. The room was the size of a broom closet with a little window that looked out on an air shaft. My aunt, who looked on me at all times with tears in her eyes, was waiting for my cousin Sean to pick her up. He arrived with a beautifully wrapped package and a stricken look on his face. "I went to the room down the hall," he said. "The room was empty. I thought, I thought that you were . . . discharged."

"Discharged." I laughed out loud. "Discharged? You thought I died." This was the first time I got a good laugh out of this whole thing and said the word that had been lurking around the corner of all conversations. There's no way something like this happens to you without the thought of dying taking up a good bit of your time. And a few days later I had my first real dose of it.

After I was released from the hospital this second time, my father suggested that I go to Dana Farber Cancer Center in Boston. Every time I had a test the doctors would say, "There's no sign of cancer." I guess this was both reassuring and frightening. Obviously, this was something not so easily ruled out.

"I'm getting the feeling you don't know what's wrong with me," I told the hematologist.

"That's right," he answered.

"What I'm really getting is the feeling that you've never seen this before," I continued.

"I haven't," he answered. "And neither has anybody else so far," he added.

Up until now I had been concentrating on what it was not and hadn't really focused on what it might be. And now I was being told that nobody knew. This was a little more than I could understand. My hematologist also thought going to Dana Farber was a great idea.

But nobody could tell me why I was going. "For testing," was what we all said to one another. But early in the morning of the day of the flight to Boston I woke up and understood I was going to find out if I was going to die. What I and everyone else really feared was that something was hiding in my body. That was why I was going to Dana Farber, where I would be given every test imaginable to see if they could uncover what it was.

I remember that May morning so clearly. By myself, the early light filtering through the window and my wet hair clinging to the back of my shirt, I sat at a desk facing the wall, read postcards and invitations tacked on the bulletin board and asked myself, Am I Gilda Radner?

Am I going along thinking this is going to end and I'm going to get better when what's happening is that I'm dying right here and now, I thought. I loved Gilda, someone I didn't know, and that's what happened to her. In my own case the only thing keeping me alive was blood transfusions, and I was aware this was not an ideal situation.

I know that facing death and actually dying are two very different things, but I really handled the first one well. I understood death was a real possibility and was now prepared for it. You'd like to think that great drama unfolds during these moments, but it doesn't. It's more a shrugging of the shoulders and a Hey, whattya gonna do. It was a short conversation, no more dramatic than standing at the deli counter debating whether to go for the turkey or corned beef sandwich. Nothing major transpired, no great white light beckoning at the end of the tunnel, no awe-inspiring insight, just a plain old This might not go my way. But it was also one of my life's truly luxurious moments. In an instant I learned everything I needed to know about myself.

It doesn't mean that when it gets down to it I'm not gonna cry or scream or beg to live, but it means that I understood it might not go my way, that you take what you get.

The morning began as I walked through the doors of the Dana Farber Cancer Center into a world that welcomes you with arms open. I know how that sounds, but that's the way it is. Right from the start, someone takes care of you and helps oversee each step of your day. And you have a whole host of activities, sort of a day camp for the cancer set. My first step was an interview with Dr. Robert Mayer. His nurse asked if I wanted to see him alone, but I said it was fine to have my father and stepmother with me.

We sat in chairs facing Dr. Mayer, a good-looking, easygoing guy. He had a pen and a sheet of paper in front of him with boxes and blanks and room for notation. The doctor started rattling off a list of questions. "Name? Age? Sex? Marital status?" I answered them as quickly as he asked. Then he moved on to question No. 5. "Have you ever been pregnant?"

Busted, I thought, but "Yes," I answered. Had I hesitated, it would have been the same as answering.

"I told you," my stepmother, Ronnie Eldridge, said to my father, who said to me, "I'll kill you." Apparently late at night my father had taken to having long debates with Ronnie about abortion. She had told him that as the father of two daughters it was best for him not to adopt too strident a position because there was the possibility that one of his daughters had had or might one day have an abortion. Here I was, the sitting duck.

Once that was in the open, no other secrets seemed particularly important. By the time the doctor got to "What drugs have you taken?" I shrugged and laughed. "I grew up in the seventies," I answered. "I'd probably be better with colors than names."

"Well, let's try."

"Quaaludes, black beauties, pot, cocaine, any prescription in every parent's medicine chest . . ."

As the list grew, my stepmother chimed in, "What about LSD?"

I mumbled, "Maybe a few times. But it's been years since I've done anything," I added. "Except pot."

"That Billy Jelin," my father said of my best friend, who liked to smoke a little reefer.

"Dad, I was smoking pot long before I met Billy," I said. Leave it to parents. Thirty-two years old and they still want to blame your bad behavior on your friends.

Later, momentarily alone with the doctor in the examining room, I confided in Dr. Mayer. "I lied about the LSD. It was a little more than a few times. But that was fifteen years ago. I'm a serious person now. I really am." Dr. Mayer assured me he doubted my past drug history was related to my problem. "Otherwise we'd be seeing a lot more like you."

After a general examination, which included a lot of hole poking, a nurse walked in with a big tray covered in blue paper, carrying it like someone delivering a pizza. I immediately turned my head away. The implements of torture, the needles for a bone marrow exam. From the very first time, back on that first day at the hematologist's, something told me not to look and I hadn't. This was now my third bone marrow exam, and so far I had never seen the tools unwrapped.

I knew now how filled with fear and how sick I really was during the first exam because it didn't hurt very much. Well, let me tell you, that never happened again. The brain is a beautiful thing. It blocks out what it can't deal with, and mine has completely blocked the memory of the pain. I can tell you that during each bone marrow exam, as they stuck huge needles into either my right or left hipbone, I would rhythmically beat the opposite leg on the examining table and take long breaths in and out like a son of a bitch. When the nurse held down my leg, I said, "This is my system. It works for me." She then let go and I resumed my beat as I felt this tremendous pressure on my hip.

My next activities included a chest X ray and my very first trip to an infusion room. The room reminded me of an airplane, with row after row of big comfortable seats filled with passengers all hooked to IV bags and bottles. Off to the front of the room were stretchers with the moaners on them. I looked about and thought eloquently, Holy shit.

The bald gentleman seated next to me said, "What kind of cancer you got?" by way of a greeting. "I don't have cancer," I answered testily. By now I was a little weepy but in that stoic Greta Garbo kind of way. Again, a nurse with a basketful of clanking vials came my way. "We just need a few blood samples," she said as she rubbed my forearm in search of a good vein. I figured they'd need a gusher, as I counted over a dozen vials of various sizes and with different-colored caps. Still afraid of needles, I turned my head aside as the nurse went in for the kill. My eyes fastened on another nurse, who took a needle attached to an IV and stuck it in the bald man's chest. Oh my God, he gets his treatment right in his heart, exploded in my head. Later, when I repeated this, I learned the man had a catheter connected to a vein in his chest.

"Bad veins," my own nurse said of me. Finally, when all the vials were full of the commodity I had in short supply, I was dismissed. "The doctor wants me to take samples from the family members with you," she said. Aside from my father, my youngest brother, Christopher, a college student from Boston, was with us. "What for?" I asked.

"To type for a bone marrow transplant," she replied.

"Oh." Everyone wants a little drama in his or her life, but sometimes enough is enough. I'd about reached my limit. "Sure, I'll send them in." My stepmother was fortunately out of the loop on this one. After this, I was given a few hours off. "Go out and have lunch," my counselor suggested. Even I, the human garbage can, couldn't work up much of an appetite.

When we returned for the second meeting with Dr. Mayer, he was armed with the preliminary results of the morning's testing. "I can ninety-five percent assure you, you don't have cancer" were his first words. I got to experience about three seconds of relief before he continued, "But we don't know what's wrong with you." All he could tell me was that something was killing off my red blood cells as they were released from my bone marrow. What or why was a complete mystery. It would take weeks and in some cases months before the results of many of the tests came back. In labs on the floor above us, researchers were going to grow my cells outside my own bone marrow, in other people's marrow, run tests to determine if some hidden lurking cancer was waiting to be uncovered and other tests that I spaced out on as Dr. Mayer discussed them with me. That was OK because my father had out his reporter's notebook and was scribbling away. He wouldn't miss a thing.

Dr. Mayer had already called my hematologist in New

York, and they had discussed putting me on a high dose of steroids. Maybe that would work.

"So, you've never seen this before?" I asked.

"No," Dr. Mayer answered. He'd had one patient once with something similar, but no, nothing exactly like it.

My day ended on the shuttle from Boston, where I sat back in my seat slightly relieved that I didn't have cancer and totally bewildered that nobody knew what was wrong with me. It just didn't seem possible. And it had not gone unnoticed by me that so far nobody had really answered the question of whether I was going to live or die.

The Perfect Formula
for Washing Whites

I'm really sorry that it wasn't cancer or your spleen," my family doctor said over the telephone. "Because then we could have treated you with chemotherapy or removed your spleen," he added matter-of-factly. "Now we don't know what we're dealing with." Given the two alternatives he offered, I didn't mind the not knowing. Cancer was better? And what's with these guys wanting to cut out my innards? I had never given it much thought before, but I now found I was quite attached to my organs. And when they start cutting out body parts, no-body's got to tell me that is not a good sign. My family doctor ended the conversation on a hopeful note. "Something like this may very likely turn into cancer in ten or fifteen years," he said. So at least he had something to look forward to.

When I hung up the phone, completely stunned by the conversation, I decided never to talk to him again.

"Can you believe he said that to me? Can you believe it?" I said to my friend Peter Johnson, whom I called immediately. During college, now a decade ago, Peter had successfully fought Hodgkin's disease, a form of lymphoma. He had offered himself as my informal guide through the medical system. Peter's tone told me no, he was not surprised. "It's beyond him now," Peter said. "Just deal with the hematologist and forget what he said."

The situation struck me as so odd. This doctor had known me for more than fifteen years and had hardly ever seen me because in my whole life I had never been sick. I never even got colds. So until a few months before, nothing had ever been wrong with me, and now I was trying to cope with something major. He also knew my mother had died at fifty of cancer and that maybe it was a sensitive subject with me. This was one of my first encounters with truly astoundingly insensitive behavior by a doctor, but hardly the last.

In the meantime I had started on the steroids. Daily, I took eight 10 mg pills of prednisone and three 20 mg pills of another steriod called Danocrine. It was delightful. Right from the start I established a pattern. Essentially, I was crazed throughout the day, pretty much speeding my brains out, something I never liked to do in my drug days, and then crashing at precisely 11 P.M. and then waking at about 1:45 in the morning for the next day. I couldn't sleep any more than that, but always felt as if I'd slept a solid eight hours. Prednisone is one hell of a drug. When your day starts at two o'clock in the morning, you get pretty clever at devising things to do. And that was when I perfected my formula for washing whites. There was just something I loved about doing laundry in the middle of the night, the *chug a chug chug* of the wash cycle, the hard *ssssss* of the rinse and the fast whir of the spin against a noiseless backdrop. And I got obsessed with the idea of never having any dirty clothes, so even if I had only a T-shirt and a pair of socks, in the washer they went. Environmentalists would be appalled by the water I wasted in this period. And here, for the very first time, I am divulging my formula for perfect whites every time. Like a cake recipe, it must be followed exactly.

The Perfect Formula for Washing Whites

1. Use Shout on any spots. In my case that's coffee stains.
2. Put washer on hot cycle and mix in regular amount of powdered detergent, never liquid, with about a half cup of Clorox bleach (yes, it must be Clorox, who knows why. In the detergent department, my preference is Tide).
3. Place only pure white clothes, not even any naturals or creams, just whites in washer. Do not overstuff, two half-full loads are much better than one jam-packed one.
4. Let the clothes soak for twenty minutes, poking them around a bit.
5. Run through on full cycle.
6. When the cycle is through, leave clothes in washer and put in a small amount of detergent and run them through a second cycle.
7. Then place in dryer with Bounce. Again, never overstuff.
8. Fold immediately.

The reason this formula uses only a little bleach is that presumably this is how you've been washing the clothes since they were new. Bleach used consistently in small amounts is quite effective and doesn't destroy the material the way bombarding clothes with bleach does.

If the clothes are already yellowed or stained, this formula won't work.

The second washing is an added kick and rids your clothes of any bleach odor.

What it does for your clothes is keep them dazzlingly white for way longer than might otherwise be possible—as long as three years with some of my Gap T-shirts.

Folding the clothes immediately makes up for not pressing them.

I also do this with white shirts before sending them to the laundry to be pressed because I don't trust their laundering process.

When I wasn't doing laundry I was planning the perfect murder, sort of a complement to my perfect whites. The large dose of prednisone was really kicking in.

I have yet to meet anyone who has not used the words "It made me crazy" when talking about taking this drug. Mood swings, one of the side effects of this drug, should include becoming an ax murderer. For several months now I had been getting less than three hours of sleep each night. I was on the highest dose of this drug possible and therefore not accountable for my actions. I planned to use this as part of my defense. The person I planned to kill was the doctor who had savaged my arm that day of the second CAT scan.

I planned to park in front of the town house where he practiced. When he came out I would floor the pedal and pin him to the front of the building. I flirted with the idea of pretending it was an accident, but I figured a good detective would find a record that I'd been treated there. So I decided to admit it and use prednisone as my defense. I could find doctors, nurses and other patients who would attest to the negative side effects of this most powerful drug. For months on end I smiled warmly whenever I daydreamed about the murder. Then I hit upon a glitch. As much as I try to deny it, I am basically a decent person. I cannot murder anyone, no matter how much the individual deserves it. I find this greatly upsetting, but it is a sad fact. Especially since I had this perfect plan. Maybe someone else can use it.

With the rest of my time, I worked, diligently answered my mail, sent in every single piece of paper requested by my insurance company, but first copied each one. And I was a person who carries letters with no stamps on them in the bottom of my knapsack until they're so beat up it's a joke to mail them. Manic is probably a good description of my behavior while on steroids.

Plus, for the first three months of my illness I was held hostage by my father, who would not even let me visit my apartment for fear that something in it had caused this illness. Different doctors had speculated that perhaps I had had a viral or toxic reaction to something. I had recently been both in Italy and on the small Caribbean island of Montserrat, so my best friend's father, who at the time was the governor of New York, put me in touch with the state's commissioner of health, Dr. David Axelrod. He started our conversation with an assault.

"Didn't you notice that you weren't getting your periods?" he asked accusingly. With my blood count so low when I first got sick, I did not menstruate.

"They were light for a couple of months and then by the last month when I didn't get it I was really too sick to notice," I answered lamely. What I wanted to say was Hey, bud, I was fuckin' thrilled not to have a heavy period for the first time in twenty years, something you wouldn't know a thing about. However, Dr. Axelrod did contact physicians and hospitals in all the places I'd visited to see if they'd seen anyone like me. He came up empty-handed, but as he'd really tried, I couldn't dislike him as much as I wanted to.

My father's search for the cause then turned to my apartment building's air-filtration system—but it was odd that none of the other thousand or so tenants had experienced any difficulty. My father's next apartment theory centered on my couch.

"My couch?" I asked.

"You don't know," he barked. "You got sick right after you got it."

The reason he knew so much about the couch was that when it was delivered to my building it couldn't make it round a bend in the hallway to the elevator. When I bought it the guy had said to get the elevator dimensions, which I did and they were not a problem. But nobody had foreseen this new problem, and on the day of delivery from California, the guys ultimately had to give up and take the couch to a factory in Long Island City. I was given the name and number of a problem solver, who, for five hundred dollars, would remove one arm so the couch would fit and then put it back together and restitch the fabric and it would be impossible to tell anything had been done. Since I knew of no alternative, that was what I did. It was cold and rainy on the day of delivery, and I sort of lost it because the couch was already months late and I had no place to sit in the living room. I probably was also just starting to not feel well at this point. So I think I cracked up a little when I was on the phone with my father.

As for the couch being a suspect in this crime committed on my body, I personally was ruling it out, understanding that a little insanity on a parent's part is to be expected when a child is sick. And I was thrust into the role of child. I'm sure my father secretly thought I'd somehow brought this illness on myself and was too irresponsible to be on my own. After a few months at his house, I could tell that unless I took great initiative he'd be redecorating the back bedroom in pink and calling it little Rosemary's room. It was going to take some clever maneuvering for me to get out of there.

Before I could make my break, I had to convince my father I felt well, which I did. Constant blood tests showed the steroids were working extremely well. My body was adjusting to them and I had regained almost all the strength I'd lost during my decline over the winter. I was still in constant communication with doctors and saw my hematologist on a weekly basis.

Essentially, the steroids suppressed what was out of whack in my immune system and let my bone marrow make the red blood cells. My red blood cell count was then brought up to a normal level. Of course, I was a raving out-of-my-mind maniac, but that seemed a small price to pay. My hematologist and Dr. Mayer hoped that after an extended period on the steroids, perhaps even a year, they would wean me off slowly, and that my own system would continue to work without them.

I had been warned that you can gain an enormous amount of weight on steroids, so I was unbelievably careful about everything I ate and exercised a lot. But there is nothing you can do about the face. They call it "moon face" and that's the best way to describe it. My face got swollen and round, and it looked as if I weighed 220 pounds, though I weighed 100 pounds less. All right, 90. In addition, you get overactive oil glands, which produce acne. I was devastated the first time I saw a picture of myself. I could fool myself a little looking in the mirror, but the picture was truly horrifying.

In addition, Danocrine, which is a strong male hormone, produced some delightful black hair along my jawline. "We'll get it waxed," my stepmother offered, but I just plucked it out. The doctor reassured me that it would disappear the minute I stopped taking the steroids. The Danocrine, however, did one thing I loved. It made me flat-chested. I have always had big breasts and have always hated them. If you're not too tall, as I am, they always make you look a good ten pounds heavier than you are. You have to buy shirts and jackets in sizes larger than will fit your shoulders and the rest of your body just to accommodate them, and when you exercise you have to wear a bra made of tempered steel to hold them in place. You can never wear a little T-shirt or little anything because all you see is breasts. I also don't buy that most guys are so into them. I think that is mostly a myth a few men perpetuate. I find nothing sexy about them and was thrilled the moment they were gone. It was heaven on earth for me. I've also always been fairly muscular, and Danocrine made me more so. It gave me great definition. If the trade-off was having to pluck little black hairs off my face I was all for it. The first thing I did was buy a bathing suit without a built-in shelf.

As I neared three months of living at my father and stepmother's, I began to plot my escape from the back bedroom. I tried hinting and taking little steps, such as disregarding my father's orders to stay away from my evil apartment, but it did no good. He ignored the subtleties, so finally I summoned my courage and announced, "I'm going home." It did not go over well, but I told him I felt fine, we would see each other at least once a week at the doctor's, perhaps more often, and talk every day. My friend Abigail lived three floors away from me, my brother Kevin three avenues away, and my sister, the career criminal, around the corner. I had things covered. My father fought me, but my stepmother, who liked me just fine but wouldn't mind a little of her own space, was all for it. So with the stealth of a thief, I slipped out of there and back to my own apartment.

At this time I still had a thriving professional life. Several years before, I had stayed at a friend's beach house in the room that had been her brother's when he was growing up. It was one of those rooms in which time had stood still. All the pictures and books were from his preteen years, a good fifteen years before. On the shelf, a great cover illustration attracted my eye and I began reading this book called *The Teddy Bear Habit*, a little kid's adventure story that took place in Greenwich Village. Though the story was set in the late sixties it was also timeless. I fell in love with this book, and imitating a Hollywood hot shot, I picked up the phone, called my brother Kevin, who knew a lot more about this stuff than I did, and said, "Let's buy it."

Two years, two thousand phone calls, twenty thousand dollars' worth of lawyers and another twenty thousand dollars in option fees and whatever, my brother and I owned the book. I think it was good that when I first picked up the phone I'd had no idea what I was talking about because I would never have gone through with it. Then it took another two years and I've blocked out how many thousands of dollars to find someone who would finance the film. My brother called every studio and independent film company while I honed the script until it was nearly perfect. And, of course, I quit my job as a features reporter at the *Daily News* because I had developed deep disdain for celebrity interviews and a weekly paycheck. I can chart my whole life's course by the stupid moves I've made. Finally, in the spring of 1989, right when I got sick, it all came together. A small company that had made three $5 million movies committed about $4 million to make ours. Kevin and I went on a letter-writing campaign and managed to put together a wacky cast out of nearly no money. I remember George Carlin's manager shaking his head and saying, "It's going to cost us money to work for you," and it was the truth. For almost no money, we assembled a cast that included Sam Waterston, Jonathan Winters, George Carlin and Roger Daltrey from The Who. This was about as great as work can get, and when filming began I was in full steroid pump and ready for everything. Except for the one thing that happened.

Three weeks and $2 million into filming, the group who financed the movie abruptly halted production. On a Friday evening, after the last shot of the day, it was announced there would be no more money. Apparently, there had been no return on any of the money they'd invested in the other films, and they had made it clear to the man running the company for them that when their initial investment ran out they would not put in any more money unless they saw some sign of success with the previous films. Their previous movies were garbage and nobody would buy them, and the investors remained true to their word and shut us down. The man who headed the company knew this all along, but thought he could cajole more money out of them. The worst part, by far, was that our original budget was $1.8 million, but the man heading the company told us the investors had twice that amount, so we should revise the budget upward. And as a result we were left with a half-finished movie. All these years later it's still a sad subject for me, and I hope someday we can do it again. It's not that we've been idle these six years; it took a good three years or so to determine who owned the project— we or the investors—and a lot of money neither my brother nor I could afford. And now, while we both do other things, we quietly search around to get it going again. Of course, neither of us got paid for our work because we had stupidly deferred our salaries.

So this put me in a really good position in the summer of 1989. I was suffering from an unknown illness, I had blown off my job, dropped out of the Mikhail Baryshnikov movie and had not gotten paid for my own movie. The year before, I had walked into an apartment whose rent was out of my league even when I was rockin' and rollin'. In addition, I had never gotten around to paying the IRS the money I owed them, and they were starting to hassle me. If it can be screwed up or I can screw it up, look for me right in the center of the storm. It's this incredible knack I have. Somebody smarter would call it a curse.

Because I am so sensible and grounded, I responded to all this by getting on an airplane and flying to Italy for a trip I could not afford. To me, this was the smartest thing I could do. Nobody could find me there.

Abigail and I set up camp for a few days at an incredibly expensive hotel we had visited the summer before. We had been the only couple there who were not young honeymooners or older men with second wives. So when we pulled up to Il Pellicano, a hotel built into the rocks overlooking the Mediter- ranean, they treated us like returning family. We also got a kick out of the fact that everyone clearly thought we were a lesbian couple, while we talked incessantly to each other about someday coming to one of these places with a man. Over the years, Abigail and I have spent so much time together at romantic resorts that we are now a great source of information for our friends who are couples. We have actually designed the itineraries for several honeymoons.

We hung in the sun and ate sumptuous lunches on the terrace, and it was there I discovered what is meant by an insatiable appetite on steroids. Let me preface this with the fact that I once actually retrieved a piece of chocolate cake a few hours after I'd thrown it in the kitchen wastebasket. Washed it right down with swigs of milk from the container. But for the first three months on steroids I was so afraid of a weight gain—my lifelong problem anyway—that I had eaten very carefully. Here, with as much steak and lobster, pasta, bread and oil, wine and cheese you could eat, I never stopped. From the beginning of lunch to the end, without a break, I averaged roughly an hour and a half straight. Five hours later I was pumped and ready to go into the port and start again. Generally, I finished the day with a large gelato. I continued this way for the entire ten days in Italy, including a few when we stayed with friends. Their housekeeper loved to feed people, and with a table of ten she always started with me and gave me way more than anyone else. With my now extra-muscular body combined with a few pounds of fat, I was looking like a defenseman for the Detroit Lions. The moon face was now stretched to capacity, the acne was going strong, and when I ate too much salt my hands and feet swelled. Abigail said my feet looked as if they had elephantiasis. All in all, I was a pretty attractive sight.

After my European jaunt, I settled back into trying to eke out a living. Kevin and I sold an idea for a TV pilot, so we got paid to develop it. On my own, I got hired to write an Afterschool Special for ABC. The woman in charge at the time was trying to break the mold, so she wanted me to write a script about a kid from Brooklyn who goes to Northern Ireland. I kept asking the woman where this would be filmed, as I knew the network would never agree to the price or the risk of filming in Northern Ireland. She said they would be willing to film there, but as the months wore on it became apparent that was not the case. She then told me she'd been told certain parts of New Jersey looked like Northern Ireland, and I made a mental note to collect my final paycheck the day I turned in the script. I couldn't resist mentioning that they drove on the other side of the road because she wanted lots of car and tank scenes and I thought it might be a little difficult to get right-hand-drive vehicles in New Jersey. She didn't think it was a problem, and I realized she was out of her mind. All I wanted to do was write a nice little TV movie for teens, maybe with a little more humor than the usual, and I got stuck with someone who's got to reinvent the process. Her job ended before the script was finished. The woman who took over complimented me on my work and said there was no way they were going to even try to make this film. I said I knew. But I did get paid.

The reason I had waved good-bye to the Mikhail Baryshnikov project was that Misha got a little worried about his real-life image as a ladies' man and wanted that part of the script toned down. Since the project was titled "The Man Who Drove Women Crazy," that seemed to make as much sense as substituting Jersey City for Belfast. There, too, I made sure to collect my paycheck before blowing out of there.

So as the months progressed nothing changed with my health—I continued to sleep for two hours and forty-five minutes each night and wash whites in the midnight hour, and my life seemed to be one long, steady descent into hell.

More of the Same

The days perfectly reflected exactly where my life was leading. Late autumn days of slushy gray light that slipped into a heavy winter darkness. After my last meeting at ABC, I stood on the corner of West Sixty-fifth Street waiting for the crowded crosstown bus with a feeling of such despair I was worthy of a role in a Dostoevsky novel. I had nowhere to go. Though I was working as hard as I could, everything I touched was a disaster. I was spending my off-hours as a guinea pig in various doctors' labs, had had at least five bone marrow tests since the spring, had had my blood samples and history sent all over the country and even the world, and nothing. Many doctors wanted to talk with me, but I was getting less and less interested. I was getting good at detecting who was merely trying to be helpful and who could really help. Over the winter, my hematologist had tried to wean me off the steroids, hoping that my own body would kick in and start producing those red blood cells. But when the dose dropped below what is called a "therapeutic dose," my red blood cell count dropped dramatically, so the hematologist immediately pumped me back up to the original dose.

By this time, in the waiting room and in living rooms, I had started to gather some medical information. A whole new world was opening before me. The world of the sick. I stood on the sidelines, not wanting to be a member, but gleaned as much information as I could. And one thing I learned was that some people were on this steroid dose for brief periods of time, but my dose was much higher than most people's and, as the months now rolled toward a year, for a much longer period than that of anyone else I encountered. The hematologist explained that staying on this dose was not an ideal situation because aside from the lovely side effects I was experiencing, the drugs also caused things like liver and kidney damage. But still no one knew what was wrong with me or another way to treat it.

It was on the crosstown bus coming home from ABC that I realized there was no end in sight. This just was not going to go away, I couldn't will it to be gone and it was going to torture me by being something I could not even talk about. I was getting a little sick of saying to everyone, "Well, no, nobody really knows what's wrong with me." And, of course, I was getting phone calls from helpful friends saying, "Bob has a friend who has the exact same thing as you." I'd patiently explain I didn't think so, but was always open, and, sure enough, the illnesses had nothing to do with each other. I think I'd lasted this long by believing an end must be in sight. Now I had all my hopes based on the second time the doctor would try to wean me from the steroids. My hematologist, in consultation with several other blood experts, thought maybe he had tried to take me off the steroids too soon. So as the winter dragged on I realized that months and months of the same lay before me.

And I stopped working. Stopped working completely. I don't know why. I didn't plan it. From the time I'd landed in the hospital until now, I'd never stopped working, but now I did. Which might not have been the best thing, since I had hardly any money.

Until now, I had lived one step ahead, constantly counting on the next job to pay for my excesses. Cavalier would be a good way to describe my attitude toward money. I had always lived beyond my means, but had a great time doing so. Sure, when I look back I can say that most of the money I spent was on superfluous things, but that's just who I was. And so what. I wasn't responsible to anyone but myself, I constantly dug myself out of whatever mess I'd gotten into, so big deal that I had complete disregard for finances. Of course, I was one of those people who also had to sit by the mailbox waiting for the check to come so I could deposit it in the bank before checks started bouncing. Occasionally I missed, but only rarely.

When this is how you live, it's not exactly a good idea to stop working. But I did. I shut off my computer and refused even to look at it. I viewed it as a sort of enemy. I really didn't care about writing. I'm not exactly sure why. Part of it was I didn't feel aggressive about anything, especially not about pursuing work, and that is how you get work if you're a freelance writer. I also felt that everything I touched fell apart, which was certainly a little grandiose of me, instead of just accepting that I had been having a rocky period and could work my way through it. But I didn't have the energy to do that. And I wasn't interested enough in anything. Until this point, I had thought this illness was an aberration that would go away, but now I felt this less and less and it left me numb and uncaring. I wanted work and the rest of the world to go away. I was tired and had no concentration and there was no one single thing in the world I wanted to write about. I felt betrayed by everything. I fell into a routine of reading, watching soap operas and hanging with my other unemployed friends, of whom I had many. Like drug addicts, people who don't work have a way of finding one another.

My father, as ever, was completely supportive. He called at 7 A.M. every morning and yelled at me. He has always driven me crazy about work. We have completely different approaches, but since he is the one who is far more successful, he has always hit me over the head that his is the better way. It is for him. Not for me. I, on the other hand, am much happier, more well rounded, less *egocentric*, all traits for which he has absolutely no respect. If he had a mantra, it would be "J.B. No. 1." And, of course, he can disregard the petty details of day-to-day living because he has had a woman backing him up since he was twenty-four, his entire adult life and the real span of his career. So nothing infuriated him more than my not working. He was also constantly trying to think of ways to get rid of my illness, and I could tell he thought that if I worked hard maybe I could make it go away. Since this all began, he had never missed one doctor's visit. On those days he never yelled at me, so it was a nice reprieve. But it was also the start of my feeling guilty for being sick. He'd give me those looks or actually say "Why can't this be me?" and I'd end up feeling so horrible for doing this to him. He had been devastated by my mother's death, something from which he will never recover, and now this. On top of it, my mother and I shared the same name and the truly wonderful parts of who I am all come from her. So we'd be sitting in the doctor's waiting room for my weekly blood test and my father would glance at me with one of those looks, and I'd just want to die. My father was trying so hard, but his response is always the same when he can't get a clear answer—he just keeps coming back and back and back with more probing questions. But the problem here was there were no clear answers, only murky guesses about what lay in store for the future. He also storms around all over the place, and he just didn't get that the same person he was trying to protect, whose problem he was trying so hard to solve, was also the person he was attacking out of frustration. And I didn't have the energy for it.

At this time, he was also helping to support me both knowingly and unknowingly. Money was getting tighter and tighter. Because I had thought this certainly would end, but then again wasn't sure, and thought that of course I'd get my work life back on track but was doing nothing about it, I changed very little in my life. I wasn't out buying clothes or spending money in fancy restaurants, but did nothing to change my overhead, which was after all my former life, something I thought I had to hang on to. And each month loomed the ridiculous rent, which I could no longer afford and was paying later and later into the month. My friend Suzanne taught me the trick of paying the phone company partial amounts to keep them from turning off the phone. She told me to do the same with the electric company. I blew it a few times with the phone company, which was OK because when they cut off your service you could still get incoming calls for ten days, so nobody knew. The drag was they charged thirty-six dollars to resume service, and that was a little tough for me to come up with. My father was throwing me a check for a few hundred dollars here and there, but, of course I had not been honest about my finances, so the amounts were never enough. That's not to say I didn't appreciate each one.

He was supporting me in a way he didn't know about when he told me to charge my steroid prescriptions at his pharmacy. These prescriptions totaled about six hundred dollars per month. My insurance reimbursed me 100 percent for the drugs—a fact my father was aware of—but we had a tacit understanding that he would never see the money. The only problem was it took about three months for the insurance company to reimburse me, and I got deeper and deeper in the hole.

I borrowed money from two good friends, but only enough to keep the bill collectors one step back. There was no way I could be comfortable taking money when I knew I couldn't pay it back. So nobody really knew my exact circumstances, and when questioned directly, I always lied.

Fortunately, as a year rolled around and nothing changed with my illness, I got a temporary reprieve in my finances in the form of a friend who moved to New York and sublet my apartment for four months. So now all I was was homeless. The good part was that another of my friends was traveling from late spring through early summer and let me stay at her house on the beach. At this time, both in the city and at the beach, I was living on no more than five dollars a day. My sole mode of transportation was my bicycle. I ate a bagel for breakfast, rarely had lunch and at night made either pasta with tomato sauce or pasta with garlic, oil and, if I'd just gotten a prescription reimbursement check, some broccoli. It was because I had no money that I made my first real friend in the sick world. Mrs. Rose. We'd made eye contact in the doctor's waiting room. She was always perfectly put together in Adolfo suits matched by beautiful bags and shoes. She was slim, attractive and appeared to be in her late sixties. Her stomach was swollen, and since everything about her said she was a woman who would not allow herself to have a big belly, I knew that was her problem. She later told me it was a problem with retaining fluids, and I guessed it was cancer-related, but she didn't discuss it much. I don't always catch on too quickly, but very early on it became clear to me that most problems of the blood are cancer-related.

Mrs. Rose and I both had Monday-morning appointments at 9 A.M. On a rainy day when I couldn't ride my bike but had to walk to the doctor, Mrs. Rose had her driver pull over on Madison Avenue. She stuck her head out the window and asked if I wanted a ride. On icy winter mornings when I couldn't ride my bike, Mrs. Rose looked for me and would pick me up. Somehow I think she suspected more about the state of my finances than I let on. The one thing I learned about her that I loved was that she and her husband were big gamblers and had frequented casinos from Deauville to Monte Carlo. She had an edge to her, unlike most society matrons.

Nothing much more than this passed between us, but Mrs. Rose and I were allies in this little world. When she missed a few appointments, a nurse told me Mrs. Rose was in the hospital. When I didn't see her again, the nurse told me she had died. Without ever saying it, she and I had both understood the stakes in the game we were playing.

In October of 1990, a year and a half after I'd first gotten sick, the hematologist had given up on steroids as a cure or even as a continuing way of treatment. The second attempt to wean me off had been unsuccessful and I had now been on the steroids much longer than was considered advisable. My hematologist had been in contact with other doctors and researchers, including Dr. Mayer in Boston, and had decided to try intravenous gamma globulin. The dose was based on my weight, a tough number to get out of me. The hematologist said whether it worked or not was a "crapshoot," but that if it worked it could be a cure.

For five hours a day for five days straight I sat in a room in the doctor's office known as the infusion room with a clear liquid dripping into my arm from pint-sized glass bottles. Three bottles a day, fifteen bottles in all.

In the small room six of us sat in Naugahyde chairs placed around the walls. The other patients were all getting chemo-therapy, which generally took no more than an hour, so the occupants of the five other seats changed with great rapidity. One woman walked in carrying an empty five-pound coffee tin. She didn't speak English, but I immediately caught on to what she planned to do with the tin and was comforted when the nurse explained to her daughter, "If your mother thinks she's going to be sick, tell me and I'll take her to the bath-room. She can't use that in here." She pointed to the coffee can. An old woman unwrapped a hot dog with sauerkraut; the smell permeated the room and made me want to gag. Leo, who sat across from me, announced, "I'm going to beat this," and for some unknown reason those words made me cringe. I have prayed, made deals with God, tried to become one with my illness, done whatever it takes to get through each day, but I have never uttered those words. Right from the start there was something about them that spelled sure doom to me.

For eight weeks following the gamma globulin treatment my red blood cell count remained high, and I felt that maybe something had finally worked. The hematologist was elated.

But the gamma globulin had and had not worked. After two months my red blood cell count began to drift down. My hematologist was somewhat dismayed, but said at least now there was something with no side effects that worked for a fairly long time.

When I realized the gamma globulin was not a cure but only another uncharted course of treatment, and an extraordinarily expensive one at that, I completely folded. I could feel my insides shift and the foundation give way. I'd seen it on TV when they show buildings being blown up. There's a moment when the building sways a little but remains a structure, sort of fighting to stand, but then crumbles in a heap. Only a building gets to stay demolished; I had to rebuild myself. In a way this setback helped me to settle into things. But what's the point of having something like this happen to you if you don't get to be a little dramatic once in a while.

The drama over, I settled into a routine that every four to six weeks for five days straight, for five hours each day, I'd be hooked up and intravenously fed three 750 ml bottles of gamma globulin per session at a cost of roughly three thousand dollars per day. This is what it took to keep me alive.

This new treatment was covered by insurance, so that was not a problem. But a big problem was that I no longer had the prescription scam going and was now out the cash flow I had been living on. And, oh yes, the breasts were back. They reappeared almost as quickly as the black hairs on my jawline disappeared.

As the second winter of my illness set in, things fell apart. The only move I made to work was to try to get hired by a soap opera, but I didn't get the job, and anyway, my father shouted more about writing for soap operas than he did about not working at all. He found the idea appalling. I thought it wasn't a bad one, since I watched them all day.

What I found appalling was having no money. Zero. The partial-payment system of bill paying was collapsing, the IRS now wanted me to pay up the cash I owed for my wonderful foray into honesty by finally filing the year before, and the accountant, who had done all my back taxes and to whom I had paid quite a bit already and to whom I had made it clear that the second I had money I would pay the rest, was hassling me constantly.

By early March, exactly two years after I'd first gotten sick, I'd hit rock bottom. There's no other way to put it. After a day of hiding in the apartment and not answering the telephone I stepped into the elevator and there, in living Technicolor, was Sidney Poitier in a tuxedo. He had just rented an apartment, and as the elevator descended and I kept staring at him I knew one of us was living in the wrong place. I suspected it was the person who had been unable to pay her rent for the past few months. I was down to having a little lighting problem in the apartment because two of the lights required halogen bulbs that cost about twelve dollars each.

Within a few weeks, my cousin Sean and I had worked out a deal to section off an area of his living room and I would sublet the space. My friend Maria supplied the boxes and tape from her husband's business, so I was spared that expense. My brother Kevin could store some of my furniture, and the rest my brother Patrick could use. I was actually surprised my sister didn't come around to filch a few things, but then realized she has the criminal's instinct for steering clear of sinking ships. Actually, she had stopped by a few months back and borrowed some of my checks, which she forged. But they didn't clear; my days of a positive bank account were over.

So it was in my underlit apartment on a high floor with magnificent views that I sat on a gray Thursday in March, systematically packing away the boxes that contained my life. Dressed in the gray cashmere pullover and gray flannel trousers, an outfit that symbolized to me that I had once been somebody, I took my hair out of a ponytail, but didn't bother to brush my hair. I was looking forward to going to the theater and having dinner with friends, and I had actually amassed the great fortune of eighty dollars, money that now was not going to pay bills.

This was the state of my affairs on the night I met Tony Dunne. And the broad strokes of my medical story were what I told him on the night of our third date as we sat in a little Italian restaurant on Houston Street after seeing *La Femme Nikita*. And though I was very direct about the medical part of my tale, I neglected to tell any of my financial story. A man can take just so much.

"OK," Tony Dunne said when I finished my story.

"OK?" I asked, my face hiding none of my confusion and my mind thinking, That's why this guy's dating you. He's a moron. "I don't think you understand."

"Oh, I understand," he said. "I heard a little of the story before and now you've told me the rest."

Then we left the restaurant and ended up on the island in the middle of the street trying to catch a cab. I stood there wondering what happens next when a taxi pulled up. "Get in," Tony said, and I was confused because we lived in different directions. "Come over for a while."

So on the night when I thought we would shake hands and part cordially, he kissed me. And I knew this was the person I was going to spend the rest of my life with. I did not doubt it for a second. But what we did not know then was that everything I had been through to this point had been the easy part.

End of Part One

Stirrings

A bad movie would cut to a montage at this point in the story. Soft focus on a spring Sunday afternoon as we ride bikes around lower Manhattan, resting in Battery Park as a strong wind blows off the Hudson River and beautiful boats cross the harbor with the Statue of Liberty and Ellis Island as a backdrop. Holding hands in coffee shops and days spent standing in front of a roaring Atlantic Ocean followed by warm candlelight dinners with caring friends. I'm sure I've seen this in several Barbra Streisand movies, the part where I usually want to throw up and my friend Suzanne is crying uncontrollably. Suzanne still considers *Beaches* a religious experience. I sat there and hated myself for crying. But since this was all happening to me, I was playing it up for the big screen. I was getting my nails done. My girlfriends came forth with their best wardrobes, the items no one usually wants to lend. The guy never saw me in the same thing twice. We were looking to seal a deal here.

For effect, I would say to the girls, "How would I know a

good relationship if I've never had one?" Until now, if you'd put me in a room with twelve normal guys and one ax murderer, my instinct was unfailing—I picked the killer every time. But I did know this was different. And so did every single one of my friends the instant they met Tony. It was that obvious.

Still, for some time, I kept his existence hidden from my father, Mr. Sensitivity himself. At one point during my three and a half years (though I only admit to two and three quarters) of dating nobody, my father called and said, "You're not a dyke, are you?" I laughed so hard and then answered, "No, but if I were I sure wouldn't tell you."

Then, about a month after I started seeing Tony, after a particularly grueling Monday at the doctor's office, my sister-in-law Barbara was crossing Central Park with her daughter Fiona. She ran into my father, who was distraught about how sick I'd gotten that day. Though gamma globulin has no side effects, the sheer volume I received was often tough on my body, and I sometimes got a fever, chills and nausea during treatment. Also, depending on the size of the vein my nurses were able to access, the treatments sometimes lasted hours longer than other times. This day had been a long, terrible one, and my father thought I'd go home and sit alone in my boxed-up apartment. He kept saying, "Come over to our house," and I kept replying, "I'm fine." Barbara now said to my father, "Oh, she's not going to be home tonight. She's going out with Tony Dunne. She's been doing that a lot lately."

I hadn't told my father about Tony because I wanted to see where it was going. If this small romance led nowhere, I didn't want to hear about it. And I knew my father would not respond favorably to the last name. You might think he'd like it, some literary-lion sort of thing. But my father would think I was dating some anemic offspring of a famous parent. My father has disdain for the group I refer to as "the sons and daughters of . . ." You can't blame him. It's that group of children of successful parents who do nothing but live off their famous or rich names and associate with others of similar stature and discuss how difficult it is being who they are as a way of explaining why they can't get real jobs. In my more superficial periods, of which there were a few, I have flirted with this group, so my father did have reason for his disdain.

Fortunately, Tony didn't fit into any of the characterizations. First of all, he was a nephew of . . . His own father, now retired, had been a successful executive at a large insurance company. To my father that meant he came from a family with a strong regard for a steady paycheck. Secondly, my father liked his aunt and uncle, Joan Didion and John Dunne—an extremely rare occurrence. My father likes nobody. And at exactly the same time I began dating Tony, my father met Tony's other uncle, Dominick Dunne. The two men—Dominick Dunne, the chronicler of the society set, and my father, who says in all his years as a newsman the people he needs to talk to always live on the sixth floor with a broken elevator—could not possibly be more different. But the day after my father ran into my sister-in-law in the park, he and I sat over coffee. "You know, I sat next to that Dominick Dunne on a plane from Dallas last week. He was a lovely guy." This was my father's way of introducing the topic of Tony Dunne, so I took the opportunity to say, "Yes, I met him. I've been seeing his nephew."

"Bring him around," my father said and then added, "What's he do?"

"He builds movie sets," I answered.

Movies, not music to his ears. But "builds," a big plus.

"Does he work?" My father likes to get right down to business.

"All the time. He's very successful."

That was the moment my father put aside the money for a wedding. A guy with a real job, real hours, a real paycheck. My father was more in love with the guy than I was. And the more he heard about Tony Dunne, the more he liked him. When my father relayed the news to my stepmother there was great rejoicing. Our extended family includes lawyers, TV producers, computer geniuses, and real estate entrepreneurs, but, as my father points out, "Nobody who can really do anything," a group in which he includes himself.

In these early times I mostly kept Tony to myself. I had never been somebody's girlfriend, but that's definitely what I wanted to be. And was I relishing the role, playing it to the hilt as sickly sweet as a Sandra Dee movie. Of course, I had a lot of time to perfect the part, since aside from my medical situation I was on hiatus from the working world.

I also didn't mind devoting everything I had to my relationship with Tony because this was a onetime thing. I knew from the night I stood with him on the street corner down the block from Gallagher's that I could go through this only once. I'd give him everything I had, and if it worked out, that would be my life. If it didn't, I couldn't go through it again.

Even before I got sick I was never good at dating. I just didn't get that you have to sell yourself to some stranger whom you barely know. And I was always the kind of girl guys liked to hang out with. Once, when interviewing Kevin Costner alone in a hotel room, he said to me, "I could hang out with you. You remind me of somebody I'd be friends with in high school." Jack Nicholson once tried to seduce me. I'm positive what turned him on most was that he'd never heard a chick rap basketball as well as I could.

So in my heart I never had a lot of interest in this dating stuff. Then getting sick with an unknown illness lowers your chances a lot more than passing the age of twenty-nine when we're talking the marriage market. I didn't just have a few strikes against me, I'd been ejected from the game. I was kind of thrilled. Probably the only good part of getting sick was I didn't have to go through the charade with my friends of wanting a boyfriend or dating or anything. Finally, everyone just left me alone. Even my close friend Maria knew I was too tough a sell in a competitive market. Illness is bad enough, but in the age of AIDS, an unknown blood disorder that is somehow related to your immune system does not make guys come knocking at your door to ask you out.

Then, to everyone's amazement—most of all, mine—along came Tony Dunne.

"You don't have to tell him every single thing about yourself. Especially about money," Maria advised. "And it wouldn't kill you to wear a little lipstick."

Still, while I was playing out this fairy-tale stuff, inside it felt so humiliating not to be able to show him I had a life. Just as we were getting off the ground I quietly moved into the cordoned-off section of my cousin's living room. I was hardly up for "Come on by for a visit." I remember when he dropped me off one night, it felt so awkward not asking him up. Everything about me was "used to." I used to have a job, used to be well, used to have money and an apartment. I used to be somebody, but who was I now? But something inside, which I wasn't even aware of, knew I had something to offer, something exceptional, and it was to this person. But only this person.

As I've said, I also knew I could go through this only once. My whole life was unstable, and I couldn't handle one more unknown. Right from the start I recognized this was the person for me. I had never felt this way before about someone, and I knew I never would again. I was as certain about this fact as I have ever been about anything in my life. And while I struggled to show Tony I was a worthwhile human being even though I didn't have any of the usual signs of it, like a job, money and a place to live, Tony was having the greatest time showing these things to me.

He couldn't wait for me to see his apartment. I should have figured this out when he asked me to pick him up at his place for a movie that was exactly halfway between our two homes. Since I always got lost in the West Village, as do most New Yorkers, I left with plenty of time, and hopped an E train down to Fourteenth Street. I actually found it too easily and had to hang around on the corner for a few minutes.

"There's a lot of . . . stuff," I stammered as I walked into the high-ceilinged apartment. I'm looking around at all the portraits of dead ancestors and antiques and thinking, What's with this dude. He must think he's Prince Charles or something. There was stuff everywhere. Huge paintings and oversized mirrors loomed over me from the walls, all the way up to the ceiling; an elaborate piano known as a square grand stretched along one wall, piled high with CDs on top and large baskets beneath brimming with blankets and magazines. Against another wall was a grandfather clock. Every surface had something on it, all of it old. Then there was all that real furniture, and lots of it.

My apartments have always been pretty minimal. My idea of the perfect bedroom is one with just a white bed. As I stood in front of a big leather chair with a stuffed leather pig in front of it, I stammered, "How did you get so many things in here?" But Tony was so excited about showing the place to me, he didn't notice my response. I was scared of it all.

It was exactly the same reaction I'd had as a kid when we moved out of a split level on Long Island, soon after my father put a professionally painted sign on the lawn that listed the people to whom he was not speaking that year, including all our neighbors. We moved into an old Tudor in Forest Hills. I was six years old, and in the car my mother spoke excitedly about the house and how my new bedroom had a fireplace in it. When we arrived, I was horrified. "We can't live here," I told my mother. "This house is used."

Here I was, twenty-five years later, wanting to say the same thing. And yet one of the first things the friends who put us together asked was "Have you been to his place yet? Isn't it fantastic?"

"Well, uh, yeah, you could say that" was my standard response.

When Abigail stopped by one night, she whispered to me, "It's as if a real man lived in a Ralph Lauren home." By this time I was very, very slowly coming around, getting a tiny bit comfortable in the place, especially since I thought this might become my home too. Quietly I was checking out the closet situation. I also figured I could make it a tiny bit more my style by immediately renting a storage space and clearing a lot of crap out of there, a thought I cleverly kept hidden. Right from the start, except for a few bumps, it just seemed to be headed that way, so, amazed as I was, this line of thinking was not off the wall.

As for the bumps, the first big one happened on our fourth date. I was still heavy into the picking-the-right outfit stage and knew I was madly in love because I was shaving my legs twice a day, and believe me, he was not touching them just yet. It was part of my psychological profile. On a Saturday night, sixteen days after we first met, Tony asked me to come over to his apartment at seven, a reasonable time for a Saturday night. When I arrived he was watching some aviation show and I was polite about it, and then he fell asleep and didn't wake up except for a few short moments over the next two hours. Finally, I said I was going home. By then it was raining and I splurged for a cab uptown, ordered Chinese food and sat in bed crying. When I alluded to this the next time we saw each other, Tony said, "It must be because I'm so comfortable with you."

"Get a little less comfortable" was my response. I'd say I was being myself right from the start.

The other bump came when I went away for a long weekend and left him the number where I'd be and he never called. I jumped every time I heard the phone ring, which is just the worst. No guy is worth it. After three days I finally called him and said I was pretty upset I hadn't heard from him. "I was going to wait until you got home. You said you'd be away."

That answer may seem to make sense, but it is wrong, all wrong. We were at the stage then, or at least I was, where communication was a big thing. That early stage, where you're always looking for excuses to talk to each other and stay on the phone for long periods of time, amounts that add up to what you'll later use over the course of thirty or forty years. And it wasn't just me. Tony was a part of it also. Guys don't like to admit it, but they get into that beginning phase where you do most of your getting intimate over the telephone.

But these minor snags, which my friends and I analyzed in forty in-depth conversations, including asking some guys for their views, which we then immediately discarded, amounted to nothing. Most of these early months just moved along in a smooth, steady progression, the way you imagine it might be if all went right but never truly believe you're going to experience.

To make up for falling asleep on me, Tony offered to make me dinner. When I walked into the kitchen, I spotted the ingredients for dinner on the counter. "I got a chicken recipe from my mother," he said.

"Oh, and it calls for cream of mushroom soup?"

"Something wrong with that?"

"No," I answered, thinking, I am going to die. I had never really eaten anything from cans. Growing up, I used to eat over at Leslie Marder's so I could have frozen TV dinners. My mother had this thing about cooking from scratch, and I used to ask her why I couldn't have the potatoes that came in flakes, which I had when I ate over at Lisa Hill's. But unlike antiques and used houses, by the time I was a teenager I knew about good food. So during dinner, I smiled and discreetly scraped the gray gook off the chicken and must have said ten times how good everything was. The next day when I called Tony to thank him, he said, "I told my brother Mark what I made you for dinner and he said, 'No. How could you? I can't believe you made her that.' " I realized there was hope here, but I assured him it had been just fine and, after watching Tony in the kitchen, realized his mother probably had known this dish would test Tony's limits. He's never cooked for me again.

About the time of the dinner date serious debate began among my friends about when it would be right to sleep together. I was all for holding out until we were married, not out of morals but out of fear. None of the others would go for that. Apparently, I was informed, the latest accepted norm is the sixth or seventh date, which I thought was entirely too early, but acquiesced, realizing it was going to happen sometime. I was all for avoiding it, but my hormones were going out of their minds. I was at the point where I always wanted to touch him, which makes you want to gag when you see it in other couples.

My biggest fear about sex was how bad I was at it. I had one helluva track record in this area. In college, I once had a secret affair with a guy named Keith, the most handsome guy in the school, a hockey player who had a girlfriend and a girl he was cheating on the girlfriend with. So I was No. 3. You figure this guy would be some stud, but we had the worst sex. It was like a gymnastic exercise. I knew it had to be me, especially since I had almost no experience.

Two years after we stopped seeing each other Keith called a mutual friend of ours when they were both living in San Francisco. Paula told him she was now a lesbian, but they got together anyway. "You know, it's still fun to do it with guys once in a while," Paula later told me on the phone. "But, Rosemary, why didn't you tell me. He was the worst." I broke into laughter with such relief. "I'm so glad to hear it," I said. "I just figured it had to be me." Still, the scars were already there.

I had some relationships where sex was better but never great, and then spent time with another guy whom I had to beg to have terrible sex with. Let's face it, sex was not my strong suit. I felt I had come to Tony Dunne with enough problems, so I figured I wouldn't mention this additional one.

Right on schedule, date seven, the latest accepted norm, was the night we ended up together in bed. My brain was telling me to relax, and for a nanosecond my body went along. Then, smack in the middle of the just getting really hot part, I got the worst case of stage fright, sat up and said, "I'm very sorry, but I can't do this. I am going to have to go home." Though my brain was stunned by the stupidity of this move and was sending the signal out, Boy, you do know how to blow it, the fear factor was overwhelming. I was pulling clothes off the floor and babbling an explanation while dressing and getting out of there in about forty-five seconds, while Tony calmly said, "It's OK. And you don't have to leave."

In the schlocky movie of my life, this scene would be followed by a night of lovemaking of roaring-ocean strength, but the truth is it took a good while to reach that point. But I figure I was way ahead of the game for someone who thought dirty movies were the best sex she'd ever get.

Coffee, Tea or Chemo

On the medical front things were in a stable period, though at the time I didn't know that was because I hadn't been through this before. The doctors didn't know either because they had never treated this illness before. So mostly everyone was in the dark and nobody knew what would happen next, but on the whole things were pretty calm. One week each month, five hours a day for five days, I sat in the infusion room and had bottles of gamma globulin trickle into my system.

For the first few months after I met Tony I kept this part of my life separate. I thought I should think it was a big deal for him to see me at the doctor's office, hanging out in the infusion room with the chemo crowd. It would reinforce an image of me as a sick person, which I hated, especially since for most of the month between treatments I was completely normal. But I was a sick person and this was a big part of my life, and though I kept Tony at a distance I pretended I felt his coming to the doctor's was a bigger deal than I really did. "I just don't want you to see me that way," I said, reenacting one of my B-movie roles. How I really felt was that it wasn't a big deal, and if he was going to be with me, then he was going to have to deal with it. But I had this fantasy going and taking Tony to the doctor's with me was a big dose of reality and did not fit into my Sandra Dee girlfriend role, at least not in Act One. Act Three was another story. Tony would quietly mention once in a while that he would like to come to the doctor's, but I put him off. So I went by myself and my father met me there. After two years, I had worked it so that my father didn't sit there with me the whole time during treatment, but came and went. And I had a great thing going. He brought me hardcover books, which symbolize great wealth to me. Who can afford hardcovers? And he would bring me fancy cappuccinos from Sant' Ambroeus and E.A.T., two Madison Avenue establishments whose prices are what most people use for down payments on houses.

So I would drink coffee and read. But sometimes the infusion room was a real kaffeeklatsch. We'd sit around in our BarcaLoungers and get comfortable and chitchat.

"Whatdoya got?" was the usual icebreaker.

Treatment schedules tended to overlap, so you got to know people pretty well. There was the waiter from Ratner's, the Kosher dairy restaurant on Delancey Street, where my mother and I used to eat when we weren't eating pastrami at Katz's after shopping on the Lower East Side. The waiter always fought with a professor from Columbia. When the Columbia professor collapsed in the bathroom and EMS came flying in, I knew someone else would soon be occupying his chair. This place had a high attrition rate. So when Leo, who was so goddamn boring, again uttered those fateful words, "I'm gonna beat this," to the group, I knew he was a goner.

We all were secretly guilty about how we felt when Leo bit the dust.

In both the doctor's waiting room and the infusion room, I was always subjected to "the look." The compassionate smile accompanied by a lingering gaze, which together read, "So sad. Someone so young." No matter how many times it happens, you never get used to it. It cuts right through you. It didn't help that everyone thought I had cancer. The other young people there were a lawyer in her late twenties who'd had a radical mastectomy and a very pretty woman, also in her late twenties, who had had a tumor removed from her cheek and most of the bones on the right side of her face and half her palate removed, so that side of her face was a little flat. Still, she looked pretty good. When I arrived on the scene, she had just started reconstructive surgery, but the doctors had found more cancer, and she was now back getting chemotherapy and had more surgery up ahead. I was very happy when her mother told me she had a loyal boyfriend. That kind of thing just makes you feel good. A lot of men run.

Thinking about those two women helped keep me in my place when I got heavy into my "Woe is me" act. Every time I begin feeling as if I've gotten the worst deal in the world and it completely sucks and everyone I know is much better off than I am, somebody unknowingly comes along to slap me in the face. One time, tears streaming down my face, just worn out by the whole thing, I pulled out of the doctor's lobby on my bike and nearly ran into a young guy who was pulling his contorted leg behind him. It was going to take him a half hour to get to the corner and every eye would avoid him. Those kinds of things stop you from feeling sorry for yourself pretty quickly, and I'm sure they were somebody's reminders to me.

Another time there was tortured moaning coming out of my doctor's office. Later, shaken, he told me he had had to tell a young Hasidic woman who was five months pregnant that she had tested positive for AIDS, contracted from a blood transfusion a few years before. "This is a death sentence for all of us," the woman wailed, though both her husband and baby later tested negative. Time and time again scenes such as these would be repeated whenever I felt defeated.

This was from a world from which I totally excluded Tony in the beginning, and which he went along with for a brief while. Also, I didn't want to show up with an entourage. No matter who came, my father was going to be there, and often Ronnie was with him. My father spent so much time with me you would think the guy didn't have a job. Once, there was a two-week period when he drove me crazy. We got into a fight over the phone and I wouldn't let him go to the doctor and he got so out of his mind that I had to give in. I have generally found that any fighting with my father is a failed proposition. It takes too much energy.

For the most part I saw my father in connection with a doctor's visit and then he always left me alone about other things. It was the one time I was safe. Who's going to scream at a daughter sitting there with a bottle hooked up to a tube connected to a needle in her arm? And, increasingly, getting that needle in me was my one problem in this otherwise idyllic period. And it was a huge problem. The more my bad veins got used, the worse they got. And my veins were seeing a lot of action. One time it was so hard for a doctor to find a vein he used one in my groin. That was a particularly pleasant experience. On some treatment days, my nurses would search my arms for a vein like someone looking for an obscure destination on a map. If that failed we would run my arms under hot water, slap them and tie a rubber tourniquet tightly around my arm until something, anything, popped up. "I would have failed miserably as a heroin addict," I told my nurse.

The nurses could use only the smallest of needles on me, and even then the first attempt often failed. Other times they would find a vein and, just as the relief set in, it would "blow out," which means it gets bloated like a tire and is no good. Obviously my veins are Brand X, not Goodyear.

Sometimes if it was quiet and I wanted to sit in a chair by myself and make phone calls or read, I would hang in an empty examination room. It was a break from the crowd. One afternoon I sat there by myself, my right hand resting lightly on the knee of my expensive Ronaldus Shamask khaki pants, a needle taped to the top of it. Four veins had blown out before we found a good one. Though the vein was not in a great position it was a large one, which meant it would cut down on the number of hours I had to spend there. I'd already been there for three hours.

I heard a noise down the hall, the familiar sound of heavy, fast footsteps and the crinkle of a paper bag. No matter how many times my father's been to the doctor's office, it makes him nervous, so he moves faster and talks louder. He appeared in the doorway, his hand fumbling inside the bag, trying to pull out a cappuccino and hand it to me and at the same time trying to fit his body in between my intravenous pole and the examination table. He lurched forward and spilled the coffee all over my book, my pants and the hand hooked up to the IV. It could be worse, I thought as I laughed and took the coffee from him. Still moving and apologizing, my father then crashed into my IV pole and I felt a little tug in my hand. "You hit my IV," I said, cracking up, sitting in a pool of coffee. He clutched his chest and threw himself down on the examination table, covered his eyes with his hand and moaned, "I can't believe I did it."

"I think it's OK," I comforted him.

As he lay there in anguish, I added, "I'm so glad you came by." My gaze fell to the spreading stain on my lap.

Not a reporter for the last forty years for nothing, he followed my eyes and then whipped out his credit card. "Take it. Go buy anything you want. It'll make me feel better." But this time I declined. You never want to appear greedy.

"Don't you want something to eat?" he asked, still clutching the bag from E.A.T., though I had expressly forbidden him to buy anything there because it is so expensive, but when I'm at the doctor's he shops there from guilt.

"No, I'm not exactly hungry right now," I answered, looking up at the IV, which was no longer dripping. Though I didn't want to upset him any more, I reluctantly added, "I think you knocked it out."

My hand was getting very large, as if someone were pumping it with air, sort of the Elephant Man syndrome. "I think I'll call the nurse," I said.

"I'll be fine in a moment," my father responded, attempting to lift his head from the table.

The nurse arrived, and after making sure my father was all right, she removed the needle from my hand. She applied a hot compress and said the swelling would go down in a day or two. This trauma so upset my father that he hit his head on the table with a thud. The doctor, who was walking by, stopped in to make sure my father was OK. Actually, I think his real interest was the tomato and mozzarella sandwich my father had produced from the bag.

"Go on, have a bite," my father said.

"My wife says I have to lose weight," the doctor answered.

"You're skinny. Me, I look at a cookie and gain weight," my father responded.

Was this really happening?

As they conversed, the nurse searched my hand for a vein, finding a small one, which meant I'd be there for hours longer than I had expected. But that was OK. I had company.

"Did you read my column today?" my father asked, sufficiently recovered to return to his favorite topic—himself.

"No," I answered.

"What do you mean?"

"Yesterday, you gave me this speech, so I knew you were working out your column, and then this morning I saw you talk about the same thing on a morning news program, so I got the point."

"Hmfff," he sniffed.

A long time later, when the last of the liquid had entered my body, my father announced, "You can go home and rest. I'll go work. But you have to get better. I can't take this anymore. It's taking entirely too much out of me."

Before he left, he again thrust his credit card in my hand. This was our little routine. The worse my day, the better my father treated me and the more I got. A little depressed, a little worn-out from the ordeal, a few Band-Aids on my arm, and he pressed upon me my choice of credit cards. "Go buy yourself something," he would say. "Make me feel good and spend a lot of money."

This may sound like the words of someone unable to deal with the problem at hand, but it's actually the opposite. My father innately understood there are times when you are so aware of your situation that the last thing you want to do is talk about it, that there is nowhere words can take you. What you need to do most is escape. And there is no escape in the world like shopping. First of all, when it's not your money, it's like going to Disneyland. When you're sick and you've just watched your hand blow up and have spent a great deal of your time among the dying, what could be more fun than entering a fantasy land and buying a new dress, a ridiculously expensive bar of soap, or two of an item you especially like. Also, it's a commitment to living. You think, Hey, I'm going to wear this, which means you think you're going to stick around. All of this is far more pleasurable and healthy than one more discussion of how bad your situation really is. There are times when one more word about health will cause you to tear every single strand of your hair out. All of this my father understood, which is why he insistently thrust his credit card in my hand even when I resisted.

I broke him in on purchases at the Gap, then slowly moved up the scale to Bergdorf Goodman and Barney's. I did not make many small purchases, but confined my buying to a discreet number of big-ticket items. One good Donna Karan purchase looked a lot better than ten small ones from different stores. In all things, you've got to have a system and play on the psychology of the participants. My father got off on the idea of extravagant purchases, and it wasn't so bad for me either. Not a penny in my pocket, but a $500 sweater and $260 shoes.

Actually, my financial fortune hit boom times after meeting Tony Dunne, and without any scheming on my part. I had a few bucks in my pocket and it felt good. From what I can tell, my father figured if I presented a more robust financial profile to Tony it would make me more desirable. There was something Chinese about the whole thing, sort of sweetening the deal with the promise of a dowry. I wasn't complaining because I now had $250 a week with which to wheel and deal, and let me tell you that's a long way from zero. "You could buy the guy dinner," my father advised. And I did.

I spent almost all of my allowance on Tony Dunne. Something about him wanted me to make life perfect for him. Right from the start I wanted to shield and protect him. He's this big, strong solid guy, but there's a real sensitivity in there, somebody who takes a little longer, whose mouth doesn't move ahead of all else and though seeming completely self-sufficient actually is in need of some real nurturing. Exactly the opposite of me, but, oh, was it appealing. He was like the thinking woman's football player. I would just look at him, and not even for a single second did I want to hide the way I felt.

In the beginning I did get nervous for him sometimes because he took a beat too long to answer and something about his slow, steady pace made me worry that people would think he wasn't smart. Of course, this is because I am such a jerk. Sometimes I'd even cut in and start to explain Tony's answers, as if he really needed that. As if I were some great success story who should be leading the way. But oh God, I was just so in love with this guy.

Let's Get This Show on the Road

A t this point, so much of what I knew about Tony was instinctual. It was that once-in-a-lifetime feeling that you and this person fit inside each other, that in so short a period of time you would consider anybody else a relative stranger, you are willing to give up your entire life for that person. In my case, you might say, big deal, but it was. All of a sudden the fact that I was a dropout from the real world and had what equaled a part-time job at the doctor's office no longer mattered. None of this scared Tony off, and he made it clear he completely understood what he was in for. And as much as I am the motor mouth from hell, I am also very good at conversationally getting people to tell me things—things they don't normally tell in an easy and comfortable manner. I'm a terrible interviewer in the straight sense of the word, but an unbelievable one in getting people to talk. I applied all my talents to Tony Dunne. The poor guy never had a chance.

In the very beginning I drew him out almost exclusively. He's not someone who jumps to tell his story, and he had a lot to tell, some of which I only completely understood a long time later. The most important thing, and the hardest to assess truly, was that Tony had been sober for only eight months when he met me. Eight months earlier, he built magnificent sets for the Peter Weir film *Greencard* on a heavy commitment to cocaine, vodka, pot and wine. He finished the film with great success, but believed he would die if he didn't clean up. So he talked to someone who recommended a hospital in Minnesota. Like all smart addicts, after he made the decision to go he went on one last binge, which included getting his car towed on the morning he was supposed to leave. His faithful friend Zach packed Tony off and told him he'd handle it.

Tony thought he had cleaned himself up sufficiently for the trip, but when he got in a cab at the Minnesota airport the driver turned around and said, "Rehab, huh?" Tony stayed there for the standard twenty-eight days, and whatever happened worked because what I met was a person so solid he balanced his checkbook. Tony explained this was because, just a few months before, he found uncashed checks in pockets of pants shoved in the bottom of the closet. His cluttered but organized house had been complete chaos before rehab. While Tony was gone Zach had cleaned up the entire apartment and thrown away all the drugs.

I told Tony it was good I met him after the drinking and drugs because I wouldn't have been able to handle it. I'd been around it and part of it too many times, and now I was too old and had too much else going on.

So, really, just eight short months lay between what was and what might never have been. He understood that a lot better than I did. And I instinctively knew that in a way Tony needed my support as much as I needed his. He was solid—

it's not as if one tough time would make him fall back into the abyss of abuse—but his solidity could be strengthened with support and I was the person to give it.

And falling in love was the simple part. I think Tony simply fell in love with me the way I did with him. It just happened. Two dates a week became three, and by early June, less than three months since we'd first met, I was pretty much staying at his house full-time, though I was still paying rent on my cordoned-off section of my cousin's living room. At the time, Tony was working on a Paul Schrader film with Susan Sarandon and Willem Dafoe called *Light Sleeper*. Fresh from rehab, he was working on a movie all about cocaine addicts and dealers. But hey, he was getting paid and hanging out with me at night.

And I kept drawing him out. He talked to me about his work, his crew, his motivations, his dreams and desires, the brand of motor oil he used in his car. I made this guy tell me every single thing about every single moment in his life.

And I told him about mine. And I talked to him about everything connected to being sick, letting him in on all my feelings, things that were too hard for my father, friends and family to hear, but that Tony could listen to and often help.

"You're everything I prayed for," he told me one night after my mature question: "Tell me why you like me. Tell me why you want to be with me." I am at all times so subtle.

"You're what I've been dreaming of for a long time," he answered. With all the changes in Tony's life, he said there was now room for another person, and he'd hoped he would find one. I don't think he expected it would happen so soon and move at the pace it did. But hey, you gotta go with the flow a little bit. Tony's a lot more one-step-at-a-time than I am. Sometimes a little too much so.

With all this honesty, I felt compelled to lay one thing right on the line with him. "If you think you're going to screw me over or get weird or anything like that, you have to let me know now. Whatever else happens, well, that's just the way it goes. But if it's going to be one of those 'I can't handle it right now' things, let me know now. I've got too many unknowns in my life, and I know this isn't a sure thing but I'm willing to gamble on it unless you think you're going to pull some weak shit on me or play games. It will put me over the edge and probably destroy me. You know, I'm kind of fighting for my life here." I remember the words exactly because it's one of the few times I thought about something for a long time before saying it. In general, I feel my brain is an impediment to my mouth.

"Do you think I'd be here if I were going to back out or looking to play games?" Tony asked. "I'm a little beyond that. I'm opening my whole life to you. What else do you need to know?"

When he said that, he reached for me and wrapped me in his powerful arms. I believed in him like nobody else. Tell me, do I have the makings of a great romance novelist?

And because this was all happening over the summer, there was that golden light to everything. In the bad movie of my life this part would require a lot of gel lenses and everyone would look tanned and beautiful with the late-day sun pouring in at a low angle near the horizon. They probably wouldn't get the first shot off until six in the evening, but I was writing the script, so nothing was too corny. Since nothing like this had ever happened to me before, I had to wing it on the behavior front. I would say from the June night that my friend Suzanne and I made out a wedding list, my intentions were pretty clear. But how to get this guy moving was another story entirely. So far, I had gone for complete honesty about almost everything.

"Now's the time to play some games," Maria advised me on the phone one night.

"I don't know," I answered. Just then her other phone rang and her husband, Ken, cut in and told Maria she had a call. Ken stayed on with me.

"Just do exactly what you've been doing," Ken whispered conspiratorially. "Whatever you do, don't listen to Maria. I married her despite all the elaborate games."

So I continued to be completely straightforward and increasingly uncool about my wants and desires. I don't know if it's because I found what I wanted and, like a little kid, had to grab it now or that I was more aware than others, not by choice, about how little time we sometimes have, but even though I was outwardly a tiny bit cool, inside I was moving like a bullet train. I wanted this guy something awful.

And it didn't help that everybody who met Tony just assumed he was the one. The women always got it right away. It's the eyes. They're so humane.

When I could put off Tony's meeting my father no longer, I dragged Tony to some event at Rockefeller Center. My father was into telling the story that I'd met Tony because my father had held up my picture on the David Letterman show as one of the many women in his life he was trying to marry off. He actually did that, held up pictures of me, my sister, stepsisters and some of our other single women friends, and we all got calls and one teenager from Grosse Point sent me an 8 by 10 glossy of him dressed in a tuxedo and offered to come to New York and take me out to dinner. But we know that was not how Tony met me. "I used a little literary license telling the story," my father said. You knew my father was desperate because those are words he would never use. Tony hit him back with his own language. "Yeah, you lied," Tony said. I didn't see them for the next hour and a half, and I knew right then this was both the best thing and the worst thing that could happen to me.

After my stepmother met Tony a week later, things started to accelerate. On the very first visit to their apartment, Ronnie had Tony fix the dimmer switch in the living room with the only tool known to my family—a butter knife. Tony's success left him a marked man. After that, a dinner invitation to their home meant Bring your tools. At the time, Ronnie was running for reelection as city councilwoman from Manhattan's West Side. It was now late July, and she made it clear that September was really the latest she could handle a wedding. "I don't know," I responded. "He hasn't even mentioned getting married yet." Tony was completely unaware that any of this was taking place, which is probably the way it should be. By mid-August, Ronnie was asking, "Is there a problem? Should your father and I talk to him?" Oh yes, I thought, that would be perfect, my father and stepmother asking the guy to marry me. I know they were champing at the bit to see me settled—parents can't help it—but I replied, "Give me a little more time." As in all things, my father was operating on a deadline.

On Tony's side he had a few people looking out for him as well. One afternoon I had lunch with his uncle Dominick Dunne, who was working on a piece about William Kennedy Smith, and had been told I knew someone who dated him. Quickly, he surmised without my saying so that I really didn't know enough about the alleged rape to help him. But I did know enough to get myself in serious trouble with one of my closest friends, so for once I decided to be smart and keep my mouth shut. Anybody who has ever worked for the press is the worst person to try to get information from. Because the minute you open your mouth you've already said more than you meant to. Dominick knew I was dating Tony, and soon steered the conversation to his nephew and intimated he was a gentle soul. He also told me the story of rebuilding his own life after the age of fifty and reincarnating himself as a successful author. I don't think he had any idea at the time what those words meant to me. Hell, I had another sixteen years as a loser before I had to pick up the pieces.

My other meeting with Tony's family was with his aunt and uncle Joan Didion and John Dunne. We had dinner at Shun Lee West. What I remember most is that I had to go to the bathroom so badly I thought I was going to lose my mind, but I didn't want to get up from the table because they had a great conversation flow going and I didn't want to interrupt it. They talked movie business with Tony and asked me questions about writing. John was actually aware of my work and took an interest in it. Joan, who is the size of my left arm, came across as someone with a center made of steel and fiercely protective of those she loved, who included Tony. In the best way, it was made clear they were checking me out and that so far they approved. When I finally excused myself at the end of dinner to go to the bathroom, I had to control all my muscles to walk there. I knew these were two people I would be really lucky to have in my life. When your self-esteem is virtually nonexistent, it feels good when you hold your own with people like Joan and John.

Then one evening Tony's cousin Griffin Dunne came over to Tony's apartment. He's one of those people with an incredible amount of energy who can immediately launch into a story, play all the parts, make you laugh and focus the attention on himself. He is, after all, an actor. While we sat there spontaneous thoughts erupted in my head. At any other time in my life, if you had put Tony and Griffin in the same room, I definitely would have gone for the latter. I would have thought this is what I want—fast, furiously funny, the lime-light, references to people whose last names need not be added, the works. And now, sitting there, I thought he was a great guy, but was glad when he went home and I was there alone with Tony. All of a sudden I appreciated that what I'd always thought I wanted was not for me at all. All along I had been aware that if someone had described Tony to me I would have said, "He sounds nice, but he's not for me." The thing is I had never gotten past the image of what I wanted. I'd like to say getting sick, which certainly catapulted me ahead in many areas, had also brought me this new insight. But that's not the case. I think if Tony Dunne had not been placed right in front of my face and quietly extended invisible support, I would never have known he was offering me a life that I had never dreamed of, one I didn't even know I wanted and the only one that would bring me happiness and peace. I'm sorry, there are only queer words for all of it.

My longest bad relationship once flew me to Paris for a long holiday weekend. We flew on the Concorde, stayed at the Ritz and drove a sports car to the countryside to stay at a fantastic château. And I had the worst time in my whole life. He had never treated me right, and I was so strung out at this point that the whole time I fantasized about grabbing my plane ticket and wondered if I could get to the airport before he noticed I was gone. He even took me to Chantal Thomas, a lingerie store, where I had picked out a few things, and then told me he was also going to buy these extraordinarily expen-sive intimate items for his sister as well. I cared so little that he was lying that I said I'd wait outside. As I left, the sales-woman, in silent recognition of what was going on, put a beautiful bodysuit in the bag with my purchases. Here I was, doing something out of a Danielle Steele novel and being completely miserable. I had the sense to finally get rid of the guy when we got home, but it took me a long time to let go of my image of what was important.

Once I got sick, so much changed. But I never invested a lot of time thinking about it because basically I figured either I was going to die or this was a temporary turn of events. What I didn't realize was how much I was both growing up and changing.

On the night after Griffin went home I think I finally began to understand why I loved Tony Dunne so much. Without saying it, but by showing it, he was taking me somewhere I'd never gone. I'd had the good sense to fall in love with him in the first place, but now he was telling me that if I just calmed down, stopped expecting and anticipating, I might find myself where I really belonged. And the best part, the part neither of us knew before, was the places we would bring each other.

I'm Tapping My Foot

That's all well and fine, but I am who I am and just a taste of this made me want the whole thing now, immediately, yesterday. And so, while I was going with this in all the important senses, there's no way around it. I wanted to get married.

I don't know when exactly it started in the serious sense, but once it did I knew there was no turning back. When I met Tony it was something I had completely ruled out. Now, not only was it something incredibly important to me, but very quickly it became the only thing. I tried to keep it quiet, but since that's not possible with me, one day I just blurted out, "You know, I'm not going to stick around forever." At this point we'd been together five months. "I'm not sure why or what it means, but I know I can't stay if you're not thinking that way. If you told me you would stay with me forever, but you didn't want to get married, I don't know why, but it wouldn't be all right. I couldn't stay. I don't know how this happened, but once I realized I wanted to marry you, there was nothing else." I'd say you can't get much more straight-forward than that.

"I'm not opposed to the idea," Tony answered. What an overwhelming endorsement. He then added, "Let's take a little time." I wanted to throw some hard object at him but restrained myself. Throwing things would come later. Instead I took a deep breath and knew the subject had very much been opened. Unfortunately I couldn't figure out how to get Tony to talk about something when he didn't want to, so it just lay there. But he had hardly heard the last of it from me.

As the summer wore on, we continued to spend all our time together, and I only returned to my cousin's living room to change my clothes although I was technically living there. As for the doctor, I had my routine down.

Finally, on a Friday in July, Tony had the day off and I had the last day of my treatment, so there was no way to keep him from coming. I told him he could pick me up and I pedaled uptown on my wheels, which I always left in the bike room at the doctor's office. By the time Tony arrived the rest of the crowd had vacated and I was there alone. He surveyed the scene and made a point of being completely nonchalant about the IV needle in my hand and the near-empty bottle hanging on the pole. Actually, he leaned over and stuck his hand in my shirt just to tease me a little. So there, my big secret life was finally out, and he made it clear this was no big deal to him but being a part of it was. "It's so much of your life," he said. "How could you not want me to be here?" And yet, as smoothly as this went, the next few hours held a major glitch. I have never let Tony forget it was a test he failed.

Just as we were leaving the doctor's office my father showed up and we decided to grab an espresso on Madison Avenue.

But there was the question of my prized possession, my bicycle. A beautiful, carefully maintained hunter green Cannondale mountain bike. Very understated. The only people who ever commented on my wheels were people who really knew bikes. In New York City that means the people who steal them.

I'm a city chick, and having cruised the entire New York City subway system on my own since I was twelve, my antennae go up when trouble lurks. Like the time the little punk in Central Park tried to throw me off my bike and steal it. A split second before he made his move my legs were already pumping and I left him in the dust. Always bros would pull up beside me and say, "Nice ride," with their eyes openly saying, I'd like to rip off your bike. The one time ever that I left it on the street and sat two feet away in an outdoor café a bike messenger pulled alongside it and stole the pump. I never ever locked it on the street or even let go of it for a second.

Against my better judgment, I let Tony talk me into locking the bike in his Jeep at noon on Madison Avenue. Less than three minutes later there was a commotion on the street and I went outside. The back window of Tony's Jeep was smashed and my bike was gone. A woman who saw it happen said a guy jumped out of a car cruising up Madison, smashed the window, pulled the bike out and took off on it. Tony was upset about the Jeep and went inside the café, made phone calls to get the window replaced and debated about whether to call his insurance company. He said he was very sorry about the bike. That was it, "sorry." I was devastated. And, it was my sole mode of transportation. Stealing my bike was the same as stealing the car of a traveling salesman. And the best he could come up with was "sorry." I figured his good sense would kick in at some point and he would discuss putting in for the bike to his insurance company or helping me replace it or something. But no, as the day passed, nothing. He said it was going to cost three hundred dollars to replace the Jeep's rear window. I quietly said it was going to cost over one thousand dollars to replace my bike, which meant there would be no replacement. Tony said nothing. But this was not the last he would hear on the subject. I made him wish he had bought me a new bike that very afternoon. In my mind he had done the wrong thing, and because he had to live with me that's all that mattered. I'm not a pleasant sight when I'm unhappy. And I was very unhappy.

Fortunately, I wasn't left completely wheel-less. I had a spare set, a Nishiki that was so stiff that every time I jumped a curb I could feel the vibration up to my elbows. This was the same as replacing a BMW with a Ford Fiesta. Also, there was no pride in ownership. Every day I got on this bike I felt my loss even more, and how much Tony had let me down. Soon after the bike incident, fate threw another test our way and Tony again failed big-time. It was early August, and I went to Maine for a week to stay with my friend Billy Jelin. He had sent me a round-trip plane ticket, a fact I kept to myself. While I was away Tony finished a job a few days early and decided to drive up. We hung out and had a great time inhaling lobsters and going too close to President Bush's house in Billy's boat, so the Secret Service in rubber Zodiacs had to warn us to keep our distance.

Tony suggested we drive back to New York together and that way we could spend a few days at his parents' house on Cape Cod. I had never met them and was both anxious and nervous to do so, but said it was a good idea. I also made it very clear I had to be in New York no later than that Saturday, four days later, because I was going away with Abigail. Tony said he'd get me back in time.

We drove to the Cape, and I think what was most on my mind was my mouth. My language. I kept telling myself not to curse, which is not easy for me. I'm never vulgar, but I tend to use fuck as a well-placed modifier. As we pulled up to Tony's parents perfectly appointed home and his mother dressed in crisp cottons greeted us in the driveway I knew my instincts about my mouth were right. Tony later admitted he'd never heard her curse.

Both his parents went out of their way to make me comfortable, and they succeeded as much as one can with a visitor who is trying to be on her best behavior. I knew they knew a little about me, that Tony had said I was a writer, graciously leaving out the part "who doesn't write." His parents also knew a little about my illness, but since I was tanned, fit and pumped up on gamma globulin no one could tell there was something seriously wrong with me. And since a possibly dying woman might not be Mom and Dad's dream date for their son, I played down the illness card quite a bit, although that was unnecessary. That very first evening, moments after we walked in the door we were whisked off to a dinner party at Tony's cousin's house. Our host, Michael, is the kind of guy who immediately takes care of you, kind of mentally puts his arm on your shoulder and lets you know he'll play defense as face after face of various relatives looms in front of you. At one point early in the evening, as we sat on Michael's porch overlooking the Bass River, which flows into the Atlantic, he told a hilarious story of a girl he'd been dating and how it had been six months and he felt this should be the time to be thinking about marriage, but then she'd worn Charles Jourdan high heels for a weekend on the Cape and his better instincts told him it would never work out. "You know at our age six months is all it takes. If you don't know in six months, you're not going to." Tony and I were less than a month away from the magic number six. I let Michael know I couldn't agree with him more, although I really thought it was more like six hours.

Later that night, as Tony and I tried to sleep in a twin bed in the back bedroom of his parents' house I started to cry the quiet tears of deep despair. Tony knew exactly why. "I know. Will you just give it a little time." Even if I wanted to I couldn't, but Tony didn't see that. The few days spent on the Cape passed quickly, and I knew I had made a good impression on Tony's parents. They're very calm, unintrusive in their kids' lives, supportive of whatever their children chose to do, but I suspect there was a little behind-the-scenes quiet discussion between them that their son should hold on to this girl. This was a reassuring feeling for me. And I was ready to go. But as much as I liked Tony's parents, by the end I was really worn-out by being on my best behavior. Also, I had to get home to pack. I may have left out that I was jetting off to the south of France in a few days. Especially in the worst of times, it pays to have good friends, or maybe despite my other faults I was almost always a good friend and it paid off when I most needed it. My friends Alvin and Phyllis, Abigail's parents, invited Ab and me to the south of France for ten days. First-class tickets and everything paid for.

So I had to get home by Saturday to leave for Nice on Sunday. I know, it's tough. But actually, it really was. Because on Friday Tony told me he didn't have to be at work until the middle of the following week, so he thought he'd stay and spend more time with his parents. "Fine," I said. "I can always fly home." Fly home! I had twenty cents to my name, how the hell was I going to get home. I mean, I had started this trip with my free round-trip ticket, which I told Tony I had to forfeit when we drove to the Cape, and now I had no ticket and no money. I was too embarrassed to mention this to Tony, but silently hoped he'd offer to pay for the ticket. Wrong. Not a word. A phone call revealed that the one-way ticket from Hyannis to LaGuardia cost about two hundred dollars, and after I'd made the reservation I silently freaked for the rest of the day. You'd think the guy would offer to pay for my ticket, since he was mildly aware of my financial situation and knew that I had given up my other plane ticket, though he didn't know I hadn't paid for it. But no, Tony never offered. You'd think I would have learned from the bike incident. Another test failed.

At this point, you may ask why I was so desperate to marry this guy, but I saw these as minor deficiencies, which I could easily correct. And, in the case of the plane ticket, it might have been better to tell Tony the truth, but I was too uncomfortable. Instead I told him I couldn't find my Visa and that it was the only credit card I had with me. I said I must have left it in Maine. I looked a little flaky, but what could you do.

Finally, Tony said he'd pay for the ticket.

"I'll write you a check," I offered.

"OK," he said. He actually accepted the check. Tony also advised me to call and cancel my Visa, which was pretty easy, since I didn't have one. Again, different people have had different opinions about whether or not Tony should have bought me the ticket, but since mine is the only one that matters, let's just say he was completely screwed.

So off Abigail and I flew on a trip most people couldn't even dream of. Jack Nicholson stood next to me at the luggage carousel, but didn't remember me. I didn't care that it was now five years later, and though I looked pretty good, to him I was over the hill. And he wasn't looking too hot himself, gray and pudgy, after eight hours in the air.

Abigail and I spent long, lazy days swimming in the Mediterranean, zipping around to different ports in her father's speedboat, pulling up alongside huge yachts and checking them out, dining at some restaurant on the beach in St.-Tropez, where we swam ashore while Ron Perelman, with his usual big, fat cigar in his mouth, was picked up from his cigarette boat and sat foolishly in the little dinghy the restaurant provided for those who didn't want to swim the few feet in.

In the afternoons Ab and I jogged past David Niven's pink house and then back to our hotel in tiny Beaulieu. At night we hit great restaurants with her parents and generally had an idyllic time. Until about ten o'clock at night. Then I would miss Tony in a way I had never experienced before. I'd always had wanderlust and would just pick up, hop a plane and cruise around until my money ran out without giving a thought to separation. But I'd never really had anyone to be separated from before. I'd also never thought of ten days as being very long before, but now it seemed forever. At night I ached for Tony. To shut me up, Abigail and I would jump rope on our hotel patio at midnight. The good thing about my closest friends is that they are generally as crazy as I am.

And they also know me at least as well as I know myself. They understood how much I needed a break. This trip to France was like the ultimate shopping spree. It gave me the chance to forget about my illness, to pretend I wasn't sick and not feel like a nobody with no money. I found I was capable of intelligent conversation. For a short while the whole medical world didn't exist for me. I got to be a thirty-four-year-old woman on vacation with one of her best girlfriends whose biggest problem was getting the guy to marry her. Because I am able to remember every single detail of that trip, I understand how important it must have been to me.

During a long swim one afternoon in the warm sea I felt so good, so strong and powerful, that I thought maybe my illness had gone away. I've experienced this a few times over the years, especially since doctors have said it may go away as mysteriously as it first appeared. I just felt too good to believe I was still sick, and hoped maybe my body had overcome the invader, maybe this trip was all it needed. Maybe I would go home and discover I had miraculously recovered. For this brief while, I must have chosen to take my fantasies as far as I could.

During the trip, in between lunch at the Hôtel du Cap and champagne and caviar at a sugar heiress's mansion in the hills of Villefranche, high above the Côte d'Azur, I gave a lot of thought to my relationship with Tony and determined that we had to make some progress. I was feeling increasingly awkward about staying at his house and changing at my cousin's, and I just felt I needed my own place even though I couldn't afford it. So I decided when I got home, if I had to I would sublet an apartment that had been offered to me. I had no idea how I would pay for it, which is an odd thing to be thinking about when you're sitting in the south of France and waving at a waiter for a ten-dollar bottle of water.

On my first day back, after Tony told me he had gone absolutely insane during my absence and that he'd missed me from the moment I left the Cape, I broached the subject of my living situation. It was a dead day in August, and as we sat in an empty downtown restaurant I told Tony as reticently as possible, without appearing false, that I felt uncomfortable about not having my own place and I wasn't sure what I would do, but there was a small apartment on the Upper West Side and I was thinking of taking it. Silence. A few beats. And then a second's hesitation before Tony said, "Why don't you move in with me."

He never had a chance. I would have been willing to bet anything on the outcome of this conversation, but I played it the right way. Maybe Tony had failed to come through on the bike and the plane ticket, but now he came through big-time. And I took great pride in the fact that he was blissfully unaware that he'd been set up. He actually thought it was his idea. Of course, I initially responded to his offer with "Are you sure?" but I didn't push too much. Never overplay your hand. I had my own set of keys an hour later and unpacked my clothes from France just to establish myself. And a footnote on the airplane incident, as I prefer to refer to it. Later on this same summer afternoon Tony mentioned that my check for the plane ticket had bounced. I was pretty embarrassed because the one thing I was pretty good at was not bouncing checks. I couldn't afford the twenty-dollar fee. A few days later I had scrounged together the two hundred dollars and turned the money over to Tony. He took it, a move I made sure he would regret for the rest of his life.

Once You've Got Your Foot in the Door, You're Still Nowhere

Do not think moving in slowed down in any way the marriage locomotive. I was picking up steam and there were only a few stops left before we reached our destination. Still, as September became late October and the golden leaves blew off the tree outside the living room window, nothing. Zero. Hardly a word about getting married. It was the only thing that undermined our domestic bliss. And it was blissful. I had reinvented myself as Donna Reed with a filthy mouth and an edge. Mornings found me pushing a vacuum, cleaning the bathroom and running off to the dry cleaner. Right after moving in I had told Tony he didn't need the housekeeper. It was hard to justify to myself having someone come in to clean while I wasn't working. But the bigger reason was that on the days she came it meant I had to come up with someplace to go for four or five hours. That's a little tough, especially when you're on a tight budget, so it was just easier to do it myself. And it loosened up a few bucks more for me. This is called survival of the bottom feeders.

In the afternoons I shopped for dinner, wandering the small streets of the Village and finding great little gourmet stores. Soon I took to getting Tony small gifts. When I moved in he owned only graying sweat socks—and you can imagine how I feel about that—and old T-shirts. I bought him new socks and T-shirts and, on wild shopping sprees, Gap shirts and sweaters. I loved him so much I wanted to make his life perfect and new socks were a beginning, and if that was all I could do, I would do it.

And, in my own small way, I was now loaded. I was no longer paying rent and I had my stipend from my father. And then a new source of income fell my way. Unfortunately, it also fell into the gray category between stolen and found money. Actually, it didn't fall into that category at all. I considered it straight stealing and felt pretty weird about it at the time, but I was still in a desperate situation. It all happened the first time I did the laundry. Tony's pants pockets. And shirts. I'm not talking about the stray five- or ten-dollar bill. I'm talking major money. Sometimes three, four twenties in a shirt, a few tens in his pants and plenty of stray fives and singles. A load of laundry could produce an easy one hundred fifty bucks, a few times almost twice as much. A borrowed jacket was often a gold mine. What to do? I'd say it's pretty clear what I did. My sister would have been proud. I never spent any of the money on myself. I bought flowers for the apartment, small gifts for Tony, paid for the dry cleaning and groceries. But I definitely gave Tony the impression I was paying for these things myself. Not that it mattered to him. Had I asked, Tony would have paid for them. But I didn't. Stupidly, I just wanted to avoid this whole area of conversation. And this stolen money did enable me to use my own cash to pay off minute amounts of my outstanding debts, my first move in a positive financial direction. But generally I was pretty ashamed of my behavior. What kind of person steals from the man she's in love with? Me. And what would Tony think of me if he knew?

Fortunately, the money dried up after a few months. It turned out Tony's crew had elected to get paid in cash on one particular job. But by late fall the job had ended, and he was on one where he received a check, which he deposited in the bank. I now found only the usual stray singles in his laundry.

Home life was a big adjustment. We had both lived alone for many years. There was a lot of sniffing and circling each other as we tried to establish our common ground. But I was always at a disadvantage. No matter how generous and loving a guy Tony was, whenever there was tension there was the slight hint that I was there because of his largess. I was really sensitive to it, and I responded by fighting more tenaciously. There were some really big fights. Somewhere in me was a fury that only Tony could unleash. I'm sure this did not thrill him. And it definitely caught me off guard. I think I might have been slightly outraged by my illness, by my own reaction to it, by not working and not having any money, by having put myself in such a naked position by moving in, just to bring up a few remote possibilities. I guess part of Tony's role was to deal with this. Our fights were about the usual combination of both semi-important and overtly ridiculous issues that turn into wars. My bike and the plane ticket were thrown in his face early on. I never fought fair. And early on I discovered the sheer exhilaration of smashing objects.

Late in the fall I was rinsing dishes in the sink and Tony was bugging me about something, and I must have asked him ten times to give me a break. He kept going on and on and I took a handmade ceramic coffee cup I had brought him from

France and smashed it in the sink. It was exhilarating. In the ensuing months a tumbler was thrown at a coffee table and a huge potted plant was overturned in the bedroom, and it took about two days to clean up the dirt. There must be a few other things I can't recall offhand, but a look in the kitchen cabinet might jog my memory. I later referred to this as my paring-down-the-apartment period. Some items in my path were severely injured and had to be discarded, so the apartment was kind of being redecorated. But my throwing of objects also scared the shit out of me. This was not a part of me I had seen before and I didn't like it. And our fights were not followed by any passionate making-up period. They just got worse. I'd scream and think OK, now it's over, what do you want for dinner. But Tony would just fume and fume and not talk to me, and I'd get mad all over again and make him sleep on the couch while I'd cry in the bedroom. The woman must retain the right to the bed on all occasions is my way of thinking.

I received solace from no one. I would call Maria and start to tell her about the fight and she would interrupt. "What did you do to Tony?" she'd say, the words "poor Tony" implied in her injured tone. "Nothing," I'd whine, but knew all was lost. Some of this was my own fault because I couldn't talk about Tony without getting this gooey look on my face that I would want to smack off someone else's and some B-movie look in my eyes and all I could say was how perfect he was. And, of course, in all the slugging it out, my matrimonial train was chugging along hard, which caused considerable underlying tension, as in I really wanted to strangle the guy.

Also, it took me a long time to understand Tony's different concerns, mostly because it was close to impossible to get him to open up. It was only after he got a job on a Milos Forman film called *Hell Camp* that Tony told me that the last year, the better part of our time together, had been his worst year professionally as a result of a contractual dispute between his union and the studios in L.A. The studios had launched an unofficial boycott on filming in New York. This affected not only the quality of the jobs he'd been offered but also their length and the pay. Since I met him he had built sets for some small films, television shows and commercials, and though I knew he usually worked on large feature films I didn't fully understand how stressful the year had been. The few jobs were highly coveted, and there weren't enough of them to go around. Tony was very much on edge about it. And most important, he is someone who takes tremendous pride in his work and loves to build imaginative sets that require a lot of thought and hard work to construct, and none of the jobs he'd been doing really asked for this. But of course Tony would never consider discussing any of this with me. It was only after he started work on the Milos Forman film in the fall, a sizable movie with a decent construction budget, that he told me his feelings about the last year.

On top of this, he feared that I expected too much, that I assumed he could give me anything I wanted. That was the only thing that truly hurt me. I'd never made him feel there were things I wanted that he couldn't give me because there weren't. But he thought I was suppressing the desire and it would emerge at a later date. He should have shown a little more confidence in me, but it really had nothing to do with me. It was his perception of himself. Me, I thought he was a god.

So I had my little world of cooking and cleaning, making bank deposits and organizing the apartment. There's no denying it—I was flourishing in this role. I was great at it, I

worked hard at it and it was also another way I could tell
Tony I loved him. Quite often he would say, "But I wish
you'd write," and I'd respond, "I don't want to talk about it,"
and he'd say, "Whatever you do is fine. I don't even care if
you write and don't show it to anyone, but I just think you'd
be happier," and I'd shrug and say "Maybe," and plan the
menu for dinner. By now, though, I had reached a different
level about not working. There was some movement inside
me, something telling me I was no longer just shutting off, that
I was actually on to something. I didn't know what it was, but
there was enough of the reporter in me to sense that something
was up. But it was too unclear for me to verbalize or even
have a coherent thought about it, so I kept it to myself. I
needed to create a sane, somewhat orderly world around me
so that I could handle the chaos caused by my illness. I also
needed to do something really well so I could feel a little
worthwhile. I had my doubts about work, but not about my
abilities with a rag and Endust.

My not writing didn't really bother Tony, who understood
that to pressure me was the worst thing to do. Unfortunately,
it didn't go as smoothly with my father, who called our house
every day to yell at me for letting my talent slip away. I felt
like telling him I made a mean red sauce, but he would never
get it.

At first I found what worried Tony only through fights,
and that was not a pleasant system. Most of what worried him
was why he was reticent about marriage. Though his concerns
were sensible—job security and money—I considered them
insignificant. I had no idea if I even had the luxury of a future,
so how could he ask me to think these things mattered.

Then, three weeks after he started on the Milos Forman
film, just as he was seeing a brighter future, the movie shut

down. Am I a curse or what? Worse, Tony had turned down an even bigger job because he had verbally committed to the Forman movie, and now he had ended up with nothing.

Tony called me one afternoon and explained that the producers hadn't been able to reach an agreement with the sumo wrestlers' society in Japan, which was an integral part of the story and where much of the movie would be shot, so they had to scrap the movie. There was probably some truth to their story, but I told Tony I still bet on financing and an incredibly shitty script as factors. I may have been a deadbeat, but I still had my literary standards and read all the scripts that were sent to the house. The worst ones usually got made.

This only made Tony want to retreat further from nupital ties—I gotta call it something other than marriage, marriage, marriage, but that's what it is—but my behavior stopped his withdrawal. To me, it was not the biggest deal and we could handle it. We weren't out rocking and rolling, but we weren't starving and Tony got other work that wasn't as good and he didn't like as much, but by most people's standards he was doing fine. I said we could get through it, and I really did show him that things could be good despite some major disappointments. I don't mean to play them up, but I'd had a few pretty big disappointments myself.

It was only when Tony absolutely had to unburden himself that he told me how horrible it felt to go through rehab, change your entire life and work incredibly hard at it, devote your entire being to your work and have it all fuck up. Especially when Tony had been so successful before rehab, making movies on location, which was the perfect formula for losing your mind on drugs, but still moving on from big movie to big movie. He now made it clear he felt the lone responsibility for both of us, which was not the case. God forbid he had told me any of this before it was absolutely crushing him so I could have given him even more support, but he had had all of mine all along.

That was the best part of being together, the part neither of us could have anticipated. It was the people we were becoming because of each other. I was flourishing as the domestic goddess with the feather duster, but really it was about thinking more of somebody else, of feeling I had things to contribute as well as a sense of self-worth and a sense I was beginning to move in a direction, I wasn't sure what or how yet, but very slowly the apartment building inside me, which had been gutted, was now in the early stages of renovation. And Tony just needed someone to listen to him and counsel him and make him see the dark side is always there, so big deal, what are you going to do about it. Behind him at all times was my unwavering confidence, and if I do say so myself, it's a pretty incredible force.

There's a Reason People Become
Ax Murderers

S o, as you may have gathered, I wanted to get married. By December I was stark raving mad. My friend Suzanne and I even made up a preliminary guest list one night and were in deep consultation about additions and deletions. I could kill this guy.

Then came Christmas. Don't go and get some romantic notion that he proposed to me in the holiday season. Well, actually he did, but it's not how you would think. No *Sleepless in Seattle* Rainbow Room scene. Then again, she did turn him down. My story involved a pen, not a ring. And not any old pen. In our home it is referred to as THE PEN.

In the weeks before Christmas I haunted the small shops of SoHo and the Village and the big stores on the Upper East Side looking for Tony's Christmas gift. I admit I had plenty of time to do so, but still I was making a big effort. Finally, blowing my whole wad, I chose an architectural-looking clock made of brushed steel and stone, one of a kind, signed by the artist. Tony's such a craftsman and a lover of fine detail that I knew he would appreciate it.

Tony's schedule was pretty tight, so I was kind of waiting to see when he would go shopping, since he had mentioned he needed to get his family gifts. We were not spending Christmas together. He was going home and I was going to my aunt's house. No way I was going to his family's until this had become a permanent arrangement. A girl can give only so much ground.

As the final days drew near, no movement by Tony. Even when he had a couple of days off, no mention of Christmas shopping. I knew I wasn't getting a ring. It wasn't Tony's style. But I waited patiently for whatever it would be. It's not that I wanted something big or even the present, I wanted to see how he thought of me. Well, I found out.

On the day before he was to leave for the Cape, sometime around midafternoon Tony announced, "I'm going shopping." He left and I straightened up the pad and the next thing I knew he was back. "I got everything in forty-five minutes," he announced proudly. That couldn't include me, I thought, unless he already had something specific in mind, but that also is not Tony's style. Since he was leaving early the next morning, he wanted to open the gifts right away, whereas I wanted to wait for Christmas even though we would be apart. It took a few hours, but finally he wore me down.

He opened the clock first and absolutely loved it. He was a little stunned, partly because it looked way more expensive than it was. Then I opened mine. Inside a gleaming, hard black plastic case was a gleaming black pen. A Mont Blanc. An exquisite writing object. A fucking pen. To describe my dismay is impossible. Initially, I half hid it from Tony, but I was devastated. "Because you're a writer," he said. Oh thanks, I thought. I hadn't figured that. As if that made me feel better. A pen. Forget that I am someone who can hold on to a Bic for fifteen minutes at most before losing it.

I had to get out of the apartment. I made up some excuse and then walked the cold winter streets, but nothing helped. We had reached ground zero. By the time I returned to the apartment I was determined to destroy Tony. At first he knew something was up, but the more my malicious campaign progressed, the more he kept asking what was going on until we passed that point and a full-grown war was brewing. Finally, in exasperation, Tony said, "Everything was fine until I gave you the pen."

"That's right." I seethed through the tightest jaw and slammed the bedroom door, opening it only to toss him a pillow.

There was a slight truce before Tony left the next morning, but the pen stood between us. For once, every single one of my friends, both male and female, understood how I felt. I was the recipient of great sympathy. Abigail's mom, Phyllis, gave me the best practical advice. "It's good you told him," she said. "Because otherwise you'll get gifts you don't like for the rest of your life."

After Tony left for the Cape, I spent the next three days tearing apart the apartment and cleaning it in a way my German grandmother would have approved. She thought dirt was the beginning of all evil and was probably right. I dusted every corner of the place, even washed windows and Windexed mirrors. Each day I put on my uniform of Tony's sweats and a grimy T-shirt and started about my business. In the middle of this, an old girlfriend of his called, in from L.A. for the holidays and wanting to take Tony out on a round of parties. And me, I'm scrubbing this guy's fucking toilet. Dead, I thought. He is absolutely dead.

Tony knew it when he called from the Cape and I sweetly mentioned the call. He didn't even try to come up with something. He knew I was over the edge. "I told my mother about the pen," he said. "I think I understand what the problem is."

Well, goody for you, I thought, but left it unsaid.

Tony returned the day after Christmas, unshaven in grubby sweats. While we hung out on the couch in the gleaming apartment he asked, "So you want to get married?"

I took one look at him and thought, You slob. Come up with something better than this. "No," I answered primly.

"Yeah, well, think about it," he said.

Early the next morning, while still in bed, he asked me again.

"Yes," I answered. Though this clearly was not the proposal of my dreams, as I've said, never overplay your hand.

Tony never knew what hit him. While he was quietly adjusting to the idea and telling his family, the marriage juggernaut was in full force. My stepmother was working her end, Maria and Abigail were dividing up their tasks, I was figuring out dates, refining the guest list and starting to figure out where the event would be held, all of which I had already done considerable work on.

A few days later, amid faxes and phone calls, Tony started to look like a stunned deer. "Isn't this happening kind of fast?" he asked as the first engagement gift, a tea set from Matilda Cuomo, arrived. "Fast?" I replied. "Everybody's been chomping at the bit for six months. We're ready to go."

He briefly mentioned that the month of September was a good one. I gave him one look that shot him down and let him know June was the latest. Tony asked if I'd ever consider eloping. I never even had a chance to figure out how I felt about the idea because my father, his sixth sense in full gear, called literally five minutes later. "I hope you're not thinking of eloping or something like that because I would consider that an act of betrayal."

And the timing was perfect. Playing the part of the girlfriend was nearing the end of its run. I had the part down pat, so it left me too much free time. Since I was still not ready to work, I needed something. What better than to plan my wedding.

Because I don't have a mother, I was left to do it on my own, which ended up being great. My stepmother was more than willing to help, but she not only was extremely busy but wanted to give me a lot of room. My father was more than willing to pay for it, but he's not one of those fathers who are willing to go along to your fittings or to go over the menu. The only bad part was, my father would give me no parameters. He refused to discuss money, telling me, "Whatever you want." In the end it's not too difficult to figure out. It costs what it costs, which is exactly twice as much as you initially think, and that's only if you're paying close attention.

I imagine almost every woman whose mother is not alive when she is about to be married experiences the same emotions. I felt closer than ever to my mother because I knew how happy she'd be, how impressed she'd be with the man I'd chosen and with the woman I'd become. Until now, even though I'd talked about her to Tony, I was still private about my mother. In the beginning, when he'd find me buried in the couch crying I would often lie about why, embarrassed to admit that after a decade I still wanted my mother back. Finally, one time I let it out: "I want my mother. She would help me understand why this was happening to me." My mother could make me stronger and better able to deal with my fears. She had given me most of the tools necessary, but I now needed a master class, and I knew she could teach me. Yet, in a way, I often got it from people who had known her.

Even now, with regularity, I meet people who say, "I knew your mother," and their tone alone says it all and makes me feel so proud to be connected to her. In many ways, my relationship with Tony mirrors that of my parents. Nobody but my brothers and sister could know how much of my father is a result of my mother's able hand. And in my own relationship, I saw some of this gift had been passed down to me.

During all the marriage mania, Tony thought I should go to my mother's grave. I hadn't been there since her funeral, and he thought it would be good for both of us. She's in a vault because when my brother James, the only person in my family capable of dealing with the funeral arrangements, began to explain about the plot, for a reason I'll never fully understand I blurted out, "Please, don't put her in the ground. Don't put my mother in the ground." Nobody said anything, and James just handled it.

After the cemetery visit I dreamed of her. I was walking up a hill in Bantry Bay in Ireland, a place we both loved, and as I neared the road a convertible bounced along the country road—my mother and her two best friends, Mary Daly and Fat Thomas, both dead now, drove by me, smiling and waving. They didn't stop. When I woke up I believed it could mean only one thing. It wasn't time for me to come to her. Not yet, at least. I hope she'll help me when it is.

So with my mother very much on my mind, I planned my own wedding. And I really had a lot of fun and help from all my friends and family. Abigail and her mother will never be able to look again at a rolled napkin with a ribbon around it without thinking of me. For all the festivities preceding the wedding, Maria stepped up to the plate and let me know exactly how I was going to do things. She shook her head dismissively when I made fun of her behind her back and let me know that she knew better, which she did. She dragged me kicking and screaming to Tiffany's and told me what I was going to register for. I made so much fun of Sybil Connolly trays and stands that were like rich people's TV trays. As Maria marked them on the list I was thinking, "If anybody gets them for me, I'll return 'em." Maria shot me a glance. "I know what you're thinking and you're going to use them all the time." I do.

A few weeks later informal note cards with "Tony and Rosemary" engraved in gray on the top arrived. They were the first of Maria's many presents. "Informal notes are the right tone for you," she said and knew she need not tell me I'd better have my thank-yous out in considerably less time than the accepted two-week limit. The few times Maria can get a tight rein on me, she does, and then openly relishes the torture. And though Maria's five years younger than I am, as she loves to point out, she has helped me a lot in my rocky path to adulthood.

I registered for my place settings and silver at Barney's, and the best part was getting Tony to come. He made it next to impossible, but once there, he put together on a table an eclectic and perfect arrangement, including napkins and place mats. He never looked at a price, but invariably chose the most expensive items. But he really did it right and with much more flair than I could have—not all the stuff matching but complementary. He's got unbelievable style, but none of the usual prissy stuff that usually comes along with it, although as we left the store I made a point of torturing him with "You can tell me, you're gay, right. I know your secret." After all, he subscribed to *Architectural Digest* and *HG* and bought design magazines in French. What more proof do you need? In Queens you could be hanged for such behavior. "Now I know why you live in the West Village," I continued.

"Sometimes you are so unbelievably stupid," Tony responded. I beamed up at him. Ah, true love. But that's what it was. And that is why I can openly ridicule Tony and make major points of his shortcomings—always remember my bike. But I also could never last more than a few nights away from him, which ultimately ended in his limiting my calls home after seven o'clock to five on the few occasions I went anywhere without him. When the sun went down, I'd be the kid at the sleepover who wanted to go home. All I wanted to do was talk about Tony, couldn't make it through a dinner without him unless I made at least one phone call home. The support he gave me made it so much easier for me to start to recover from the blow of this devastating illness. I had this strong person behind me who loved me and understood me and knew both the attractive and the unattractive things about me and still wanted to be with me. But let's get on to more important things. The ENGAGEMENT RING. And if you think he failed before, be prepared.

Tony was still reeling from the devastating hit the New York film industry had taken from the boycott. I also didn't know that he tends to take the bleakest perspective, though I suspected as much. Simply put, he was nervous about money. Don't mix this up with being cheap, because he is the furthest thing from that, which I discovered with increasing delight. But he doesn't like to get in over his head. So we had a discussion right after his memorable marriage proposal about a ring.

"I don't need one," I said.

"Are you sure?" Tony asked. I assured him I was.

"What do you need a ring for?" my father asked. "What's that got to do with anything?"

"I agree," I answered.

In the meantime, practically every person who heard I was

engaged would ask, "Can I see the ring?" It didn't help that my close friend Perri got engaged at exactly the same time and was sporting a rock. I knew it was all so petty and meaningless, but when Abigail and Maria set a March date for my engagement party, a bomb exploded.

"You said you didn't want one," Tony said from his foxhole.

"I didn't mean it. I thought I did, but I didn't and you should have known that" was my response. Time to get good and nasty. "I've never been through this before. You have. So you should have known. Did you get your first wife a ring?" Now he was mortally wounded, but the death blow was next. "Didn't one of your dead ancestors leave some jewels or something that you can take a stone out of and give me?"

With a fear-filled face, Tony revealed he had given his first wife a stone from a piece of his grandmother's jewelry. You can imagine my pleased response to this information. "And you're so tough to please," Tony said. "I knew you wouldn't be happy with some chip."

"That's right," I answered.

"You've got to help me out," he pleaded.

"You're on your own" was my response and gave him the deadline of the engagement party. I was not going to it with nothing on my finger.

In the middle of all this marriage mania came a little medical surprise. As I sat with my legs hanging over the side of the examination table my doctor said, "We've had limited success with hormonal therapy. So I think we should try some chemical therapy."

"Chemical therapy?" a tiny voice eked out. If you ever want to know what it feels like to be struck by lightning, try this.

"Chemotherapy," he explained.

My mind just went numb. In order to hold on at all, my brain fixed on one point. "Will I lose my hair?" I asked.

"Not on the size doses we'll try. They're very small."

I shook my head and seemed pretty focused, so the doctor continued. I didn't hear another word. I just sat there and felt like a *Star Trek* character transported to some simultaneous universe. Because this was definitely another world with another Rosemary's life. Not mine. A few days later I confided in my nurse that I hadn't heard a word the doctor said after "no hair loss." She said she completely understood. She was in the room with us and was pretty shocked also. From the first day in almost every instance, even when they're younger than I am, my nurses have looked after me as if I were their only charge and they take a lot of what happens to me personally. But Ann explained that the doctor had said he would start me off on oral doses of the least toxic chemotherapies. A world-renowned hematologist in Genoa, Italy, believed he had had a female patient with a condition similar to mine. In connection with a doctor from the Dana Farber Cancer Center in Boston, my doctor decided to start me off on Cyclosporine. I was told little about the drug. Before I got to read the little explanation that came with the prescription, the pharmacist, who had been trying to pinpoint what was wrong with me, shot out his finger and announced elatedly. "I finally got it. You're getting an organ transplant!" My face said it all. "Well, that's one of the main uses of the drug," he continued, deeply disappointed.

"Maybe next time," I comforted him.

I don't remember much about the drug except that I experienced no side effects and it didn't work. The next drug was Cytoxan. I say that's one nasty name. Again, nothing. And I

did cheat and tell Tony it made my back ache, so he gave me
lots of massages. He's great at it and can go for a long time.
Believe me, that's more important than going for a long time
during sex.

I think mostly I craved Tony's attention, so I played it up. I
didn't know that soon after I'd get too much of it. Our third
time at the plate with the chemo drugs found me getting an
injection of methotrexate, another comforting name. Why
don't they just kill me now. Once, during this period Tony
and I were in the car with his father, me in the back. They
were talking about someone with cancer and his father said,
"Once they start with chemotherapy it's all over. You're a
goner." Tony said that these days a lot of people survive, and
I sat in the backseat cracking up. I still can only laugh when I
think of this, but later told Tony, "Break your father in gently
about the chemo," which got Tony giggling because we both
knew his father is incapable of saying a hurtful word to anyone and would feel awful about something he said even if it
had provided one of my favorite moments in this whole illness.

The first sign that methotrexate was the most serious of the
chemos was that I got it by injection. You'd think with all this
poking of veins with butterfly needles and pricking my fingers
and hacking away at my bone marrow I'd be used to needles.
But I'm not. And especially not shots. My nurse thought it
was hilarious, but every time she came near me with the needle I flinched, and finally I told her to get the other nurse to
hold my arm, which is the way it had always been done since I
was a kid. Of course, the shot is nothing.

I went home and made spaghetti with a spicy red sauce,
and Tony and I ate too much of it. He had just worked eight
days straight on a TV show and a commercial on the side and
was slightly catatonic with a heavy week in front of him. We

hung out and went to bed. At around one o'clock I woke from a deep sleep, sat up and realized I was going to be sick. I rushed to the bathroom, where, well, let's say it became very red. Tony appeared behind me and held my hair back, which really won my heart. In between getting sick I apologized, but he just told me to be quiet and held my hair and rubbed my back. Finally I said I was ready to go back to bed. Exactly fifteen minutes later, I was sick again and in between fits of nausea told Tony, "Stay in bed. Stay in bed," because he was in such a catatonic state that we kept bumping into each other as he tried to help me. He couldn't keep his eyes open. There was nothing he could do anyway, and at all times I needed a clear path to the bathroom. By now there wasn't anything left in my stomach. I wet my lips with water and went back to bed. And almost exactly fifteen minutes later I was sick again. And fifteen minutes after that. And fifteen minutes after that. I think after a while it might have been a half hour in between, but it was pretty much all the time, and Tony would lift his head from the pillow and try to get up but couldn't. And I didn't want him to because I was now making noises that I didn't know where they were coming from—there was nothing in my body—and they could have taped the sounds it was emitting for some *Exorcist* sequel. They were wild.

Finally by two or so in the morning I was so weak and my stomach in such pain that I had to crawl to the bathroom. On one return trip I crawled to the side of the bed, shook Tony and whispered, "Coke."

He yelled from the kitchen, "How about Diet Coke?" and I nearly lost my mind. "No. It has to be Coke."

He started to get dressed, but then remembered I had a little display of Coke bottles on the bar and he popped a few open. A few sips, a moment of euphoria and then I got sick. But the Coke was by the side of the bed. Tony tucked me in, placed a towel on top of the blanket and set up a garbage pail with a plastic liner by the side of the bed. Before he passed out again he told me. "Just relax and don't worry if you can't make it to the bathroom." The most I managed was two sips of Coke. Tony had to leave at 6 A.M. and said, "I can't leave you here by yourself." I wasn't getting sick anymore, I was now lying on my back moaning. I had lost count after trip twelve to the bathroom, but my guess is sixteen times in total. Tony called my father, who came down immediately, and a few hours later we called the doctor, who had never mentioned severe nausea as one of the drug's side effects. He said the dose I was on was so low I shouldn't have had any reaction. My father stayed until about 10 A.M., when he casually mentioned that he had been on his way to Denver when Tony called and thought maybe he would go now if someone else could come over. Abigail came by at eleven and fed me a few bites of a bagel and a Coke. I got sick one last time and then managed to fall asleep for the afternoon and woke later feeling purged, including in the Catholic sense of free from sin, but better. This was Monday, and it took until Wednesday for me to have any strength and until Friday before I was relatively better. That gave me two pretty good days before I got the injection again.

This time after they gave me the shot I got an intravenous dose of an anti-nausea miracle drug called Zofran. It worked well for almost everyone. I found out in the middle of the night that everyone did not include me. It wasn't as bad as the first time, but it still was in a league I'd never known before. The rest of the week proceeded along the lines of the first, and so did the one that followed. Finally, the doctor decided I should take the dose in a pill form. I took the dose on a Monday and that night everything was fine. Nothing. No nausea. It was unbelievable. The following night I ate Chinese dumplings for dinner and guess what? Let it suffice to say it was pretty bad, and at this point I had now been sick in every receptacle in our home, both with or without running water.

A moment here on the aesthetic of throwing up. I don't understand why people opt for the toilet, which is sort of foul, when the sink is much more desirable. Quickly remove the stopper, brace your hands on the side, get your head down deep, and you can picture the rest. Afterward, run the water and quickly wipe the sink with Soft Scrub and a sponge. You can later run the sponge through the dishwasher with Cascade. I just find this way considerably more agreeable, and I've had quite a bit of experience.

And Tony was a champ. He kept saying to me, "We'll get through it." Most times I'd respond appreciatively, but every once in a while I'd be so worn-out that my only answer was "Fuck you. We're not going to get through anything. It's me this is happening to, and I'll smash you in the face if you tell me you know how I feel." On these occasions Tony just rubbed my back in warm circles a little longer than usual. Oh yes, have I failed to mention the drug also caused hair to grow on my ears? I mean, Michael Landon in *I Was a Teenage Werewolf*. I was pretty unhappy. When I showed them to my stepmother she said, "We'll get them waxed." The doctor said the minimum length of time I should take the drug was a few months. For the three months doctors tried this drug, I would be fine on the day of treatment, violently ill the next day, mildly nauseated for the next two days, get back my strength the next day and have one good day before the next round. And the worst part was that for a brief second it showed signs of working, which made the doctor reluctant to abandon it. I had roughly two days a week when I could really function. Only to Tony did I confide that if this was the one thing that was going to work I didn't think I could handle it. I also continued to get intravenous gamma globulin, only with greater and greater frequency.

Early on, the doctor asked me quietly, clearing his throat a few times, if I could find some marijuana. It helps a lot of chemo patients with the nausea. "I've spent the better part of my adult life avoiding finding it," I answered. And it worked great. A few hits of pot, a couple of slugs of Classic Coke, and I was on top of the world. Well actually, just off the floor. I always get mad when these moron legislators who have never had to take toxic drugs say there's no proof that pot is an antidote to nausea and therefore should not be made available to chemo patients. They actually refer to the results experienced by patients as "anecdotal," which I find offensive. I've heard many people with much worse treatments than mine say that it is the only thing that enables them to eat. But I need no more proof than my own body. The tiniest bit of reefer alleviated almost all the nausea. My favorite was when my father called at night Tony would say, "Oh, she's hanging out getting stoned."

The only good part of all this was that I could easily slide into tight black jeans. I've always been a healthy eater, a big one, but healthy. Now the only foods I wanted was junk. On one car ride I got a craving so bad I made Tony stop at a highway service station and I came out with a few Cokes, Fritos, a Hershey almond bar and a Häagen-Dazs ice cream bar. Some nights I had Coke and chocolate cake for dinner, sometimes coffee ice cream and Yodels. I hadn't eaten some of the food in twenty years, but it was what I wanted. When I made him stop and get me a shake at McDonald's I knew some really weird shit was happening to my body. Just when I was starting to look good and nasty—kind of like how Patti Smith used to when she was always falling off the stage—and wanted to give up, the doctor said the minimal benefits from the drug didn't warrant my continuing to take it. Fortunately, the hair on my ears went away almost immediately after I stopped taking the drug.

I remember almost all the details of the three months that I took methotrexate, but it was only after going through some old medical bills that I could pinpoint those months from January—welcome to the New Year—to just a few weeks before my March engagement party. I think that's because it doesn't fit the flow of my wedding story and I'd rather rag on Tony about not getting me a ring than remember what else was going on at that time.

As for the ring, Tony came through in a big way. On the evening of our engagement party he handed me a handcrafted double-banded thick matte chartreuse 20k. ring with a bezel-set diamond. No prissy, traditional-looking ring for me, but one that was really sporty and I could wear all the time—I didn't want something I would wear only on nights out or special occasions. It is just perfect. OK, I did give him a few pointers and steer him to the right person, but he did the rest on his own. I think he slept for a day straight after the tension of getting through this one. When I make life hard, I make it really miserable.

And here's a little cleaning tip for you gals out there. I use an old toothbrush and polish my diamond with Crest, not the new gel kind but the paste. The gleam on the stone is as good as a professional jeweler's and you can avoid that added anxiety of an unscrupulous jeweler switching stones.

Aside from the major ring fiasco, which we know involved

many tears on my part, most of the six months between December and Saturday, June 20, 1992, at 5 P.M., when we were married, went fairly smoothly. Maybe just a smattering of smashed objects. I have never really understood what this was about and there is still some scarred furniture to help me reflect on it. The collision of two strong personalities trying to come together and form one whole was part of it. My fears about being so dependent was also a factor. And Tony's also got an intransigent side to him. The culmination of these fights happened one night when some stupid discussion about my family's inability to plan anything in advance blew up into a brawl. We had figured out that all our fights followed similar patterns that we should try to break. My answer was that we should go into separate rooms for a while. I went into the bedroom and Tony made himself a power shake and sat in the living room. And he wouldn't shut up. I came back in and sat on the couch and quietly told him the deal was we would back off, but he had now moved on to ragging about me. I calmly picked up the big glass of chocolate shake and poured it over his head. Immediately there was great furor on his part and lots of tears on mine. I never threw anything or did anything like that ever again. I simply said to myself, This is not who I want to be. It must have taken me an hour to clean the chocolate off the chair and out of its crevices. Fortunately, the chair was leather, so it wasn't ruined. The sweater Tony wore that day was also saved by my washing skills, and to this day he'll say, "Do me a favor. Will you grab the shake sweater." At the time I gave very little thought to this fighting because I was too busy perfecting my role of fiancée. I'm what you might call a method actor in life. I spent all my time running the house and occupying myself with the wedding details while Tony earned a living.

Of course, there was the requisite round of parties, which

started with an informal dinner at my father and stepmother's
to launch the engagement. My stepsister Lucy, a lawyer for
the Justice Department, sat next to Tony. Tony asked her
about work and I overheard her say it was great, except that
she had one case where the opposing lawyer was "arrogant,"
"condescending" and "couldn't really deal with women."

"It's funny," she said unthinkingly. "He's got the same last
name as you."

"My brother's a lawyer," Tony said.

"Oh, it couldn't be. This guy's in Baltimore. . . ." By
then her trailing-off voice gave her away as she added, "And
he kind of looks like you."

So things between the two families were off to a flying start.
We all let Tony's lawyer brother from Baltimore, Rich, walk
in cold a few weeks later when Joan and John Dunne threw a
party for the two families. I further sabotaged the self-pos-
sessed Rich by asking him about work and getting him to say
the lawyer he was dealing with on a certain case was "green,"
which I immediately reported to my stepmother, who told
Lucy. "What are you doing here?" was Rich's baffled response to the sight of Lucy on the upper level of his aunt and
uncle's elegant living room. Otherwise, I must say the party
went swimmingly.

Then there was Maria and Abigail's intimate engagement
party for our closest friends. OK, mostly mine. By the way, in
this modern age when there's no really formal engagement
period, Maria and I decided it is not in good taste to ask for
engagement presents. It appears greedy, and since the point of
getting married is not the gifts, the invitation stated "No
gifts." This is our own rule of etiquette, but I think it's a good
one. The whole idea is to have a lot of fun without imposing a
financial burden on your friends. You don't want them com-

ing to your party thinking, I've gotta buy this bitch another present.

After the engagement party my friends the Pickman sisters, Peggy and Patty, threw me a shower at Patty's loft. Poor Tony was instructed that he had to pick me up at the end of the evening. Women have lots of rules. Tony arrived at a drunken bacchanalia, where there were a lot of women who had spent the last few hours examining lingerie, most of which they made fun of.

Last, there was a ladies' tea at the Lowell Hotel hosted by my friends Kristin, Suzanne and, what a surprise, Maria. She had her hand in everywhere. I think it was a combo of love, support and she was just so goddamned happy she didn't have to worry so much about me anymore. Barely a week went by when she wasn't giving me a gift or some clothes for my trousseau. "Just a little something I had," she'd say, handing me a garment with the price tag still on it. She wasn't going to rest until she'd heard those wedding vows.

And she heard them when she, Abigail and my sister, in a rare personal appearance, stood behind me on the steps of an old wooden mansion in Southampton. I was married on a golden evening following an afternoon of heavy rain and surrounded by several hundred people. My father made a touching speech, not a word of which I can remember, and then spent most of my wedding hiding because he gets shy in those situations. Ronnie took care of a lot of the socializing for him, and my closest friends and family made short remarks. I have heard most brides say they neither ate nor drank at their wedding and that they were too busy to enjoy it, but not me. In a beautiful handmade silk and lace wedding gown and new white leather Keds I rocked and rolled late into the night as the wild Atlantic pounded the shore in the background.

The ocean has been my bind to reality for my whole life. When we were kids my mother used to make us stay in it all day, so when we went home in the evening we would pass out. We always had to take our bathing suits off in the backyard because of all the sand in the lining. In the winter my mother and I sometimes drove to 116th Street in Rockaway and walked along the boardwalk and down to the ocean. And believe me, you've got to really love the ocean to go to 116th Street in Rockaway. But she did, and so do I. The Atlantic ran in her blood and in her soul and she passed it on to me. Whenever there was a big storm, we were in the car immediately. The Atlantic Ocean on the day after a hurricane was euphoria for both of us. So on the day I got married my mother was very much in attendance, and if anybody could ever love Tony Dunne more than I, it would be she.

End of Part Two

The Kramdens Take to the Highway

The honeymoon got off to a rocky start. It wasn't the fault of either of us, but my behavior did not help the situation. Maybe it didn't help that we had canceled the honeymoon and now had nowhere to go. But technically he was responsible for our not having a honeymoon. Notice, I do not place blame, I place responsibility.

A few weeks before we got married, the producer who had hired Tony on the movie that shut down called and asked him to work on *The Firm*. Most of the film would be shot in Memphis, and the producer wanted Tony to start work a week after we got married. I had planned a monthlong cross-country trip, which I happily canceled, as I understood this was a big job, as in many months and multimillion-dollar sets.

There are certain patterns to almost all movie-business jobs, one of which is that producers wait until the last minute to hire people. This means that once you get the call for a job, the weeks before you start are filled with tons of phone calls from the different departments. Basically, it's a good way of getting work out of people without having to pay for it.

After the initial call hiring Tony, the phone was suspiciously quiet. This was both unusual and unnerving. Neither of us mentioned it, and I was too caught up in other things— including the planning of a new honeymoon three days before we married—to focus on it. I came up with an abridged five-day trip to Montana, after which Tony would go straight to Memphis and I would follow.

Days before the wedding Tony tried to reach the producer but to no avail. Then, hours before the wedding, as Tony was struggling with his tie, the producer called Tony and said he had just read the script and it was terrible. Tom Cruise wasn't happy with it, and it needed significant rewriting. This is just the kind of guy I'd want at the helm of my $60 million film. I'm no industry insider, but I thought maybe one of the first things a producer might do was read the script. Just for curiosity's sake. The producer estimated the rewrite would delay the job by at least three weeks.

So four hours before I was to be married, I told Tony we could cancel Montana. I could tell he was too uptight to remove himself and I was trying to alleviate some pressure. Tony was worn-out by the stream of small jobs and was aching to work on something big and of long duration, and *The Firm* was both. He was uneasy and frustrated and wanted to stay close to home. But I had now canceled two honeymoons, and my graciousness was wearing out.

Unfortunately, I was too caught up in the way things were supposed to be. I had planned the whole wedding, which went perfectly, and now my honeymoon was all screwed up. The spoiled brat in me was rising dangerously close to the surface, and it doesn't get much uglier than that. There were a few extremely tense moments and several vicious fights on our first day of wedded bliss. It had seemed horrible to me to spend time right near where we'd gotten married, one of the world's most beautiful spots. No, that would make sense.

"Other people go to these great places and I'm going to spend mine where I've spent my whole life," I cried. I also added a few unattractive remarks like "It's not like you haven't done this before," which may be why he threw me out of the car at the Caldor's parking lot in Bridgehampton. Only when I saw Tony was near cracking did I accept an offer from my brother James and his wife, Ami, to spend five days in their romantic cottage on an East Hampton lane. For five days we acted as if we were in a place we hadn't been before. We didn't see anyone and went out to restaurants we normally shun and I kicked back a little bit.

Then, for no known reason, which was our new approach to this honeymoon, we headed for a spa in Vermont. We hung for a few days and then got restless for the open road. As I walked to our car I passed Ted Kennedy, also on his honeymoon, heading out to the courts in his tight tennis whites. Not a pretty sight.

After departing, we popped in at Billy's house in Kennebunkport and then drove up to Bar Harbor, Maine. For me, the trip was made when we passed a minimum security prison on Route 1 in the town of Thomaston. Prisoners sat at tables in the small yard, and I got that tingle of true pleasure. I've got this thing about prisons—I've always loved them, something passed down to me by my father and mother. Sometimes to make me happy we take detours to prisons. I go out of my mind at the mere mention of maximum security.

In Bar Harbor we stayed in a huge suite in a restored mansion overlooking the ocean. This was turning out OK after all. I took Tony biking in Acadia National Park and onto some off-road paths that were much more difficult than

I'd let on. With a large uphill looming before us, after we had climbed one a few moments before, Tony turned to me and I started to laugh conspiratorially. He shouted, "You bitch. You're such an unbelievable bitch," just as this whitebread family with two towheaded kids pedaled by. They looked at us as if we were animals.

While we were having the greatest time, we both noticed there hadn't been a word from the producer of *The Firm*. Tony'd put in a call to him and he hadn't returned it, and we knew that was bad. Bad as in no job. The sure sign. Without exchanging any words on the subject, we agreed it wasn't happening.

When we got home there was a message on our machine about the possibility of another job, and before Tony returned the call he found out about *The Firm*. He had committed to it, and though no one had even bothered to call him in over three weeks, he intended to honor his word. Then a friend told him the original production designer had been replaced, a new one had been hired and he was bringing in all his own people. All this had happened a few weeks before, but nobody from the film had called. This is fairly common in the film business. But I was slightly incensed that the producer hadn't bothered to call Tony. Be an adult and pick up the phone.

When Tony started to let the producer off the hook, saying, "That's how it goes," I let loose. I started by calling the guy a fucking coward. In the future I always referred to the producer as a "hired-hand lackey," which is what he is. I would go see *The Firm* only if I could use my Writers Guild card and not pay. They weren't going to get any of my money. Anytime I see this man's name on the credit list I either refuse to see the film or wait until I can see it for free. This incident brought out the main difference between me and Tony, which is that he is a nice, forgiving person, whereas I am vindictive, evil and petty.

Although nobody had called about the job, there were a couple of other messages on our machine.

"Who's this Mr. Goldstein who keeps calling?" Tony asked as he played back the tape.

"I'm not sure," I answered, my voice trailing off. Fortunately, something distracted Tony.

A few afternoons later, I picked up the phone and a slimy voice greeted me with "Congratulations on your marriage."

Mr. Goldstein. As you may have gathered, I knew exactly who he was, and his greeting helped me figure out how he had gotten my number: the wedding announcement in *The New York Times*. How many people do you think are tracked down by creditors through their wedding announcement? My luck really sucks.

I was not hiding from Mr. Goldstein. I was hiding from the IRS and quite a few others, but Mr. Goldstein was the lawyer representing my old accountant, whom I had faithfully paid the little I could toward my total bill, but he still kept harassing me for more. Everyone tells you not to hide from your creditors, but to be honest with them. The first person I tried this on was my old accountant, and he responded by siccing Mr. Goldstein on me.

Right before I met Tony, anytime I had spare money I sent it to the accountant. I roughly owed him a few thousand at this time for doing my back taxes, but had paid over four thousand dollars. Still, no matter what I sent the accountant, he said he needed more. Without warning, he unleashed Mr. Goldstein on me, whose first move was to place a lien on my bank account and take my last seven hundred dollars in the world. The lien was as bad as it gets. It was humiliating. It was also a treacherous thing to do to someone who was sick.

From that moment on I detested both the accountant and Mr. Goldstein and never sent them another penny. I also closed my bank account, and when I opened a new one I kept about forty bucks in it, and what little else I had was cash. When I moved out of my apartment and into my cousin's living room, I did a smart thing for someone on the lam. As my forwarding address I gave the post office a box number at one of those mail places. When the mood struck I would pick up the piles of bills and pay what I could. Any correspondence from Mr. Goldstein or the accountant I discarded, and instead started paying small amounts to other creditors.

But now this rat Goldstein had my new address and phone number because he'd seen my announcement in the *Times* and looked up Tony's name in the white pages.

All because of the damned announcement in the *Times*, which was all my father's idea in the first place. Right after my engagement, when my father first mentioned a wedding announcement, I was certain he was kidding. "Sure, sure," I answered and did nothing about it. Two months passed and my father again asked, "What about the *Times*?"

I looked at him. "You were serious?"

"Absolutely."

The issue was closed. "It's the only parameter he's put on this whole wedding," I said to Tony.

"It's fine with me, but no joint photo," Tony answered.

My friend Susan Wood, a photographer, said she'd take my picture, and another friend set me up with a makeup artist at the Origins counter at Saks. I was instructed to buy a few lipsticks as a thank-you. For forty-five minutes, the woman put a whole lot of stuff on me that in the end made me look as if I had on no makeup, which is the point. I have to say I looked great.

Susan and I had a great photo session. Mostly because I'm such a ham. She instructed Tony to come at the end for a few minutes so we could have some photos of ourselves. She disappeared into the bathroom with him to fix his hair a little, and when they came back we tried to loosen Tony up, but he mostly kept a puckered firing-squad expression. In the car on the way home, Tony said, "She put rouge on me," as if it were an assault on his manhood.

Once I chose the photo I slipped it, along with the relevant information, in a manila envelope and dropped it off at the *Times*. There still remained a tricky part, which I'm sure comes as no surprise. There was no way the last line of my wedding announcement was going to read, "The bridegroom's previous marriage ended in divorce," which is how the *Times* handles the situation. I hadn't been married and I was already paying enough for Tony's having been, which I pointed out to him on several occasions, but only with the utmost delicacy.

Tony's divorce had already caused one stumble on our road to the altar—the altar itself. Initially, my father had asked about our getting married in the church.

"I don't think we can," I replied. "Tony's been divorced."

"Don't be ridiculous. That's the old Catholic Church."

Sure. The old Catholic Church. A few phone calls informed me that little had changed in the Church and my religion was closing its door to me, a disappointing fact I conveyed to my closest friends.

One friend sought me out at an Easter gathering. "I hear you'd like to get married in the Church," she said.

"Yeah, but I can't because Tony's been divorced."

"There's a way," she said and explained she had close ties to a monsignor. He was soon to retire, so I would have to move fast. "He can have the marriage annulled," she explained. "What you have to do is have Tony ask his ex-wife to say she didn't want children."

"But Tony said they were young and that issue never came up."

"That's all right. It's what you have to do." My friend added that I would also need to make a ten-thousand-dollar donation to the diocese.

In other words, for me to be married in the church of the religion to which I have been more faithful than most people of my generation, it would require Tony to contact his ex-wife and ask her to lie so that he and I could then make a bribe payment of ten thousand bucks to the Church in order to have our union blessed. Why don't they just call themselves criminals and get it over with. This is a scam worthy of my sister. And the Church wonders why it's a dying institution everywhere but in the poorest of nations.

Then I learned that without the annulment the Church would never recognize my marriage, but will recognize our children if we have any. Otherwise, they'd be keeping everyone out. But I, who still had ties to the Church, would be kicked out like a dog.

Without mentioning any of this to Tony, I closed the issue by asking Judge Joan O'Dwyer, who had known me since I was a little girl, to marry us.

So by the time the wedding announcement came around I was a little impatient with Tony and his divorce status, but was still stuck with the problem of that last line of the wedding announcement. I had it all figured out. I would lie. With my easy manner, when the *Times* reporter called to confirm the information I'd sent and asked that fateful question "Have either of you been married before?" I coolly replied, "No."

You see, the *Times* does not put a line at the end of the

announcement that reads, "Neither the groom nor the bride has been married before." They say nothing. So my announcement was accurate by omission. I felt bad about lying to the guy who wrote the announcement because we had a good time talking and I got him to tell me how he could make even the biggest loser come off sounding respectable simply by his choice of words. For example, if the word, "attended" was used in connection with the person's college education, it meant he or she didn't graduate. If "until recently" came before an occupation it meant there was now no job. I began to read the announcements with a new eye. I didn't feel mine was a true lie because it didn't affect the accuracy of the story. And once the *Times* started printing announcements for people who are on Round Three and those cutesy stories highlighting couples, you figure all that old-time tradition is gone and it's a free-for-all. At least, that's how I justified it. I'm sure Arthur the Second, the *Times*'s current publisher, would agree with me if he gave it a moment's thought. However, I must refrain from offering this as one of my tips because it does involve a prevarication, and in good conscience I cannot recommend it to others. That would be irresponsible. This is a personal decision and must be made on an individual basis. Admit it, Ann Landers has nothing on me.

Perhaps I was punished for my lie in the form of Mr. Goldstein. I had never met him, but I pictured a lazy fat pig in a second-floor office on some stretch of Queens Boulevard or in some low-rent New York loser professional district like Broadway in the high twenties. If I'd intended to beat my accountant out of the money I owed, why did I continue to send payments, admittedly small amounts at irregular intervals? But after they put the lien on my bank account, when I was really left penniless, both Mr. Goldstein and my old accountant were beneath contempt.

Also, my old accountant charged a fortune and had made enough of a profit off me, so he should have just left me alone. A friend of mine, who owed money to the whole world, including me—and who could owe me money—had advised me to "negotiate."

"What do you mean?" I asked.

"Tell him what you're willing to pay. Then see what he says."

"You're kidding."

"No, I had to do it with everyone. My credit cards, department stores, even bank loans."

A world I did not know existed out there, but because of my disgust with Mr. Goldstein, when he got me on the phone I spat out, "It's a ridiculous figure. He did a bad job and charged too much and I'm only willing to pay one thousand dollars."

Without missing a beat, Mr. Goldstein came back with $1,300 if I paid within ten days.

"I'll see," I answered and hung up.

I felt like a big shot, but as I had about thirty dollars in the bank, I now had to tell Tony, who had tried to ask me about my finances on more than one occasion. For some stupid reason I felt it was too late to tell the truth. If I were truly as good as Ann Landers, I would have known it's never too late to tell the truth. I wanted to place the blame on Maria, who had stressed my need to wear lipstick over my need to be truthful about money, but that wasn't fair. Tony'd married me without the lipstick, so perhaps I should have ignored Maria's advice on the finance issue as well.

"You know that Mr. Goldstein who's been calling," I began.

Tony perked up immediately. "Yes" was his lone syllable as he waited for me to continue.

"Yeah, well, he's this lawyer who collects money."

"I had figured it was something like that."

"He represents my old accountant, who says I owe him two thousand dollars. If I pay thirteen hundred now, it'll all be over."

"So we'll pay him," Tony answered. "Why didn't you say anything?"

"I don't know. I just couldn't deal with it."

"Is there anything else I should know?"

Sure, like I'm going to tell you, I thought, but instead answered with the true conviction only a liar can muster, "Oh no, that's it." My sister would consider it an amateur performance, albeit a good one. It didn't hurt that Tony wanted to believe this, because the converse would have cost him.

We were just finishing up with Mr. G. when my brother-in-law Rich called. Tony and I were still basking in honeymoon bliss, and I figured Rich was calling to see how we were. He was. He wanted to know if I had AIDS. The news reports of a new strain of the virus, the one for which people did not test HIV positive, had prompted the phone call. I had seen a large piece about it in the *Times* a few days before. Tony assured Rich that no, that was not what was wrong with me.

I did not actually hear their discussion, but I could tell from the hushed monosyllabic "No. No. No" responses on our end that I and my illness were being discussed, so I left the room. When Tony hung up I immediately asked what his brother had wanted and he told me.

"He asked you that?" I responded, summoning up the right combination of indignation and shock. "How could he ask you that?"

"Look, I admit it was a little strange, but he was concerned."

"How do you think it makes me feel?" I left out the fact

that just days before, I had pored over the initial description of the illness in the newspapers and was assured, once again, that I did not have AIDS, a disease for which I had tested negative three different times over several years. So Rich's asking wasn't so odd, his delivery just needed work. A little clumsy, I'd say. "It's a good thing he's not a trial lawyer," I said.

"He is. And an excellent one," Tony answered.

"Guess he doesn't let his work spill over into his personal life." Fortunately the phone call about a new job made it a little easier for Tony to both brush off Rich's remarks and hand over the check for Mr. Goldstein.

It was now late July, and at that time of year New York's a pretty beat place to hang out when you have no job prospects. Sure enough, it always happens that on the deadest day the phone rings. A summer Friday. Tony was asked to begin work a week later on the film *Romeo Is Bleeding*. Though the movie was far from the scale of *The Firm*, it called for some challenging sets Tony was excited about building.

When he came home from the first meeting, I could tell he was on to a good thing. Though the script called for Lena Olin to cut off her own arm in the film, I was upbeat about the project. It wasn't a big movie, but it felt really right, and at all times I impressed that upon Tony, especially when he felt he'd lost the bigger job.

As much as I may have made poor decisions in my own life, I was really good at coaching Tony from the sidelines. It was a part of my calling in life. And my advice was simple. Work as hard as he could and do the best job inhumanly possible, and the rest would follow. I understood he needed to focus solely on work and that I should take care of everything else. And I did. It wasn't the time for me to ask for a lot of

attention. Though the unofficial boycott by Hollywood producers was unofficially over, film production was extremely
slow in New York. Jobs were scarce, and Tony needed no
distractions if he was going to do great work here and move
right into another movie, which was what we both wanted.
And so much of Tony's ego is tied up in his work and he
hadn't been getting much satisfaction for a long time. Over
time, I had paid careful attention to the mechanics of his work
and now had to prove I could put this information to use. The
main keys were make sure he had clean clothes, don't make
him go out to dinner often, keep tension at a minimum and
give him a lot of nurturing. It sounds a lot easier than it is.
And right from the start the hours were long and hard.

This Is Not Exactly What
I Had in Mind

Just as Tony was getting under way on the new job, hiring a crew and dissecting drawings, I had to make a fairly major decision on my own, though the truth is, the decision had been making itself for some time now. My veins were becoming increasingly difficult to access, the nurses were using the smallest of needles and having to resort to little veins in my hands, wrists, wherever one could be found. Sometimes nearly an hour of each treatment was spent just trying to find a vein. Then, more often than not, because gamma globulin is so thick, the little vein would blow out. And then another half hour or so would be spent looking for another vein. I was worn-out from getting poked, worn-out from leaving the doctor's office with little Band-Aids dotting my arms, worn-out from how long the procedure took because I didn't have any large veins. I had known for some time there was an alternative, but I had never really considered it until now when I had no choice.

One morning during treatment, when I was having an especially bad time, a heavyset woman ripped open her shirt and showed me a small bump on her chest, which I had seen in other patients but never really studied. She had a device called a port surgically implanted in her chest with a plastic tube inserted in a large vein. For any intravenous treatment the nurses just stuck a needle in the port, which was connected to a vein.

After the woman closed her shirt, I shrugged and looked at my nurse. She said it was a good idea. We had discussed it a number of times in the last year, but I realized now was the time. My doctor stopped by and I mentioned it to him. He returned a few minutes later and said the surgeon would see me in his office right after I finished treatment.

"Today?" I said, stunned, but relieved that my father had left earlier because it was something I wanted to do without fanfare. Something like this would make my father take to his bed for a week. I walked the few hot blocks along Fifth Avenue to the surgeon's office. When the surgeon first saw me, he was very confused because after my condition had been explained to him he had pictured a pale, lethargic person. Because my little old body keeps trying to show this disease who's stronger, I am able to operate on lower and lower blood levels and rarely look ill. I can be fairly active with a red blood cell count that would have most others in a hospital. So when this tanned picture of health walked in, the surgeon admitted that he was shocked and thought there was some misunderstanding.

After we'd talked and I apprised him of the situation with my veins and infusions, he acknowledged the severity of my problem and said this was the best thing I could do and would perform the procedure the following Monday. That seemed awfully soon, but the surgeon said he had performed roughly four thousand of these minor operations, and that it should take about half an hour and I would be treated as an outpatient, which was great because any mention of a hospital stay reduces me to immediate tears and panic. He was very nice, and I told him to expect calls from both my father and my husband. I could tell he understood completely. What he didn't know was that he was the first new doctor I had ever seen alone.

I went home and told Tony and played up the drama of the whole thing. Actually, it was pretty dramatic to me. "I'm going to have a permanent reminder that something's wrong with me," I said, which was exactly how I felt.

"Keep reminding yourself that this is a good thing, it's going to make your life much easier," Tony responded. Sometimes I'd like to punch him and all his positive energy right in the face.

"I'll be marred," I whined.

"Just think of it as your battle scars. Something to show what you've been through."

I cried for the rest of the night. Surgery. That one word stayed in my head. The good thing was I didn't have a lot of time to think about it. Late that Friday, a mid-August afternoon, I went to Mount Sinai, on upper Fifth Avenue, for a pre-operative checkup to make sure I was in good enough shape to have the procedure performed the following Monday morning at 8 A.M. The pre-op checkup took place in the oldest, dankest part of the hospital, a real 1940s prison-hospital-movie atmosphere. My first stop was a tiny room that looked like a janitor's closet, where a doctor examined me. Then I went to another room to have blood taken, and the women there could not find a vein, which did away with any thought that maybe I don't really need to do this. The woman called for a guy who handles "the really bad oncology patients who have no veins left." She really was quite nice, but sometimes the words just blow your mind.

Next, I was sent for an X ray. We were parked illegally and I got worried that the car would be towed, so I sent Tony to deal with it and said I'd meet him outside in ten minutes. What could be so bad about a chest X ray?

I was directed to some sub-basement, where I wandered the halls, and while thinking Oh, man, is this like some Kafkaesque experience, I stumbled upon a few people seated outside a door. Somebody, I don't remember who, gave me a gown and I changed in some kind of utility closet. Next to me was a horsey, yuppie couple, and, in a wheelchair, a crumpled figure with a pump and many bags of medicine attached to the pole connected to his chair and, I think, a urine bag hooked behind it. I had never really seen anything like it, and every cell in my body pleaded: Please don't let that ever be me; don't let that happen. On a stretcher was an emaciated woman moaning. My turn was last, and everyone but the woman on the stretcher had disappeared. I mentioned to the technician that the moaning woman had been left alone out there and maybe he should call someone to transport her back to her room. "Oh, she's an outpatient," he replied. "She'll leave when she's ready." An outpatient? It sure didn't look like she was going anywhere to me. I was carrying my shirt and bra with me, so when the X ray was finished, I blew out of there so quickly I changed while blindly moving down one of the deserted hallways and threw the gown on some cart.

I was back at the hospital on Monday morning at 7 A.M. Tony's best friend drove me there. That morning Tony had a meeting at work, and I figured it wasn't a good idea for him to miss it. After all, this was technically no big deal. The surgeon told me I might want to take a couple of Tylenol afterward.

This time I changed in a little locker room, and then in my gown and slippers sat on one of the plastic chairs placed against the wall. There was a small group. Nobody did much talking. A few minutes later Abigail arrived, followed soon after by my father. I was doing a lot of quiet sniffling by now. Then somebody came for me and walked me down a few hallways and ushered me through a door into a darkened space that adjoined the operating room. He pointed to a chair and left me there. All alone and in the dark. I had no idea what I was supposed to do, so I just sat there. After five minutes that seemed like five hours the anesthesiologist stopped by and spoke to me, went over the drugs he would use and had me sign a form. He said it would only be a few more minutes.

Finally, a few nurses and the assisting surgeon arrived and led me into the operating room. The surgeon arrived after I lay down on my back on the operating table with a blue paper shield blocking my view of what was taking place on the right side of my chest about three inches below my collarbone. It started smoothly, and I got some liquid painkiller through an IV. My first reaction was This feels nice, but my brain would let me get seduced only so much by the feeling. It remained alert, which proved not to be a bad thing. I wasn't aware of time at first, but once it started to seem a little long I grew more tense and more alert. "The vein shredded," I heard an assistant say, and I knew that wasn't a good thing. "Oh shit" was the next comment, convincing me just a little more. A few curses during the procedure gave me a good idea that it wasn't going the way the surgeon had anticipated. And it was starting to seem like a long time. After a third unsuccessful attempt to thread the catheter through a vein, to break the tension the surgeon announced, "This shouldn't be a surprise. Nobody knows what's wrong with her anyway."

"This is taking a little longer than we thought," he then said to me.

"Is everything all right?" I asked cautiously.

"You just don't have very good veins in your chest either. I'm going to have to look for a different spot and make two incisions instead of one." He then told someone to call down to the waiting room and let my father know everything was OK. By now I knew he would be freaking out, so that was one thing off my mind.

The anesthesiologist gave me some more drugs, and then the surgeon asked me to help him out a little and I had to hold my head in different positions. I was cool and quiet and incredibly freaked out. Finally, it was over, and the surgeon apologized and then had to run because he had several patients backed up. The whole thing had taken well over two hours.

I don't know if I was wheeled out or escorted in a wheelchair or walked, but afterward I was taken to this recovery room with lounge chairs. What I wanted was to get out of there. My head listed off to the side because it was sore and uncomfortable. My father gave me a dozen red roses, which was really nice, but I was still pretty shaky, so Abigail and I sent him to work, and she took me home in a cab and set me up in bed. By then I was extremely uncomfortable. My neck and chest hurt, and all I had was some Tylenol. For the first time ever I said I needed something else. Abigail called the surgeon's office, but he was not available and the receptionist said Tylenol was all I should need. Abigail got a little assertive and said, "I would like to speak to the doctor." In these circumstances you really need someone like her. I would have backed down and remained in incredible pain.

When the surgeon returned the call he said to me, "I'm sorry. I went into the next operation and never had a chance to change your orders. You need a lot more than Tylenol." He then told me in the thousands of procedures he had never had as many problems as he'd had with me, and if he hadn't known how much I needed the port he would have given up. He explained that he had "pushed around" a lot of the veins and the muscles in my chest and neck area, and I would be extremely sore for several days.

My brother Kevin took over for Abigail and he brought the painkillers, which helped immediately. When Tony came home from work and saw me, a stricken look was plastered across his face. "I should have been there," Tony said. I agreed, but these things take a little time to get down. I didn't want him to miss the meeting at work and thought I'd get through it without him. He figured my father'd be there, so I'd be all right. The reasoning made sense, but we had both figured wrong. My rule now is anytime I have to sign a piece of paper that reads there's a possibility I might die, my husband has to be there. Tony truly felt terrible, but explained, "I figured your father was going to be there."

"I didn't marry my father," I answered, though several of my friends disagreed with me: "You married the softer, nicer version," Maria said.

For two weeks I was depressed. Now I had a permanent reminder that all was not right with me. And all the tugging and pulling in my chest and neck had left me very sore. I had two scars and directly below my collarbone this rounded lump pushing out. A thin stream could be seen traveling through my chest because the plastic tube in the vein pushed out the skin a bit. Initially, I was in considerable pain, and I used this as an excuse for a round of self-pity. "I'm physically marred," I cried. "I'll never wear a low-cut dress again," as if this were a major problem. I got that line from my friend Perri's grandmother. A few years before, Perri and I had spent a few days with her grandmother, who wintered at the Breakers in Palm Beach. Her grandmother came down to the pool one afternoon as we were burning our chests in the hot sun. "Cover your chests," she said, and we both figured that next would come a skin-cancer rap. "Otherwise you'll get freckles and you'll never be able to wear low-cut gowns again."

Well, my low-cut gown days were over before they ever started. But the big bummer was I've got a powerful breastplate with strong, straight collarbones that I didn't mind showing off. You gotta go with your good features. Now at the gym I was slightly self-conscious about the protruding disk beneath the skin, but nobody ever noticed. For a little more self-pity, I cried to Tony, "And now I have to carry around a card because I can set off metal detectors at airports." I whined even though I thought this one was pretty funny. After the surgery I'd been sent home with a red card with the words ALERT on it that said I had this medically implanted device. The surgeon had informed me that a few people had set off metal detectors. The card also contained the number of my port, but I figured this was not a warranty number because if this product was defective I was sort of screwed. What do you do if they recall it?

This Is Not My Idea of a Good Time

After I recuperated, I settled back into a fairly regular routine of monthly gamma globulin treatments. It quickly became apparent that I had made the right decision, because treatments that had taken five to six hours now took three, and soon my schedule was reduced to five hours over three days, a savings of ten hours each month, not counting the many lost hours spent trying to find a good vein. All the nurses said my port was one of the most beautiful ones they'd ever seen. What they were referring to was its placement. For example, if it's placed in a fattier part of your chest or in a fatter person, a port can shift around when you try to stick a needle in it. Not mine. In a very short time I had bonded with my port. It made my life so much easier, the only way I could think of it was as a friend. I was proud of the many compliments it received.

At home, Tony and I settled into a nice domestic routine. Of course, to keep myself occupied, I had a scam going. That December Tony would be forty, and I wanted to throw him a surprise party. But as I had no money saved, I wasn't sure how to pull it off. Well, it couldn't have been easier. Enter the household budget. I told Tony I needed four hundred dollars a week to run the house, which included buying all the food, dry cleaning, you name it. He said, "Fine." Now, first of all, that figure was a little high to begin with. Secondly, I order all our fresh produce and pastas from Balducci's, and I paid for them with a credit card. Oh yes, as part of my rehabilitation, Tony had given me an American Express card. Somehow it never occurred to him that it was odd we had this big Balducci's bill on Amex when I had cash to run the house. A few nights a week we went out to dinner, and Tony paid. But he never once asked, "So what are you using the money for?" Basically the cost of running the house was minimal. And I was still picking up some stray bills from his coats and the laundry.

My bank account ballooned, especially as the party drew near and I thought I needed more money, so I cut further back on the household expenses and fed Tony a lot of spaghetti with tomato sauce, one of the cheapest meals I could come up with, and still he had no idea. By November I had a healthy amount in the bank, and I think Tony was beginning to suspect I had stashed away a little of my household money. He made some comment to that effect when we went out to dinner one night. "You pay," he said. "I know you can afford it." He figured I'd skimmed off a few hundred bucks. I had nearly two thousand dollars.

A couple of my pals in the infusion room helped me plan the party and the menu. I had fallen into a similar treatment schedule with a strapping man with beautiful white hair and a good-looking wife. The Minskys. Mrs. Minsky gave me some good tips on the menu. During these weeks, with my mind focused on Tony's birthday, Mr. Minsky uttered the fateful words "I'm going to beat this." Why did he have to do that? I wished he had never said those words. Didn't he know they spelled certain doom? He had lung cancer and was getting chemo and said it was going well. He looked great, so who knows.

On the surface, things were calm at the doctor's office, but down around my ankles there was a strong undertow. Fortunately, I was able to distance myself from most of it, but it did ultimately upset my entire life.

There were two big problems. One involved my very first series of gamma globulin treatments almost two years before. I had the treatments right before New York instituted a law stipulating that even if a treatment was considered experimental, if it was the only one that worked, insurance companies were required to pay for it. My case fit this description because as my illness was unknown all treatments were considered experimental.

But my first two treatments came before the law took effect, and at first the insurance company had fought paying for it and I was left with an outstanding bill of $23,000 at the doctor's office. Without my knowing it, my father had paid the bill because it made him nervous. From early on, I've been pretty sophisticated about this illness stuff, and immediately after my father's bedside chat—"This is the kind of thing that breaks families"—on my first night in the hospital, I'd been on the offensive. This is very important for anyone with a chronic or expensive illness. My best advice is isolate yourself. What I mean by that is don't let someone else pay your bills. You can borrow the money from someone, as I did from my father and Tony, but I always made sure the check had my name on it. If anyone wanted money, I wanted them to come to me, not my father. Technically, my father is not responsible for me, but I didn't want a doctor or insurance company to ever get cagey. There's a big difference between my actually paying and my showing "the ability to pay." If someone else was covering my bills, even if I had no money myself, I was showing "the ability to pay," and I was afraid if my bills ever spiraled out of control, whoever I owed money to might go after my father.

As much as I accepted his helping me out, would I want him to or could he do so if the bill was $123,000, not $23,000? In my case this is not an absurd comment because some of the procedures considered, such as a bone marrow transplant, could eat up more than the lesser amount in a morning. So I was pretty upset when my father paid the $23,000 bill without telling me and I didn't find out about it until my stepmother began trying to get the insurance company to reimburse them. But Ronnie couldn't be forthcoming to me because my father refused to discuss money, and by the time it came to my attention the bill had been paid seven months before.

In the meantime the insurance company had agreed to reimburse me for the first treatment, and the secretary at the doctor's office responsible for dealing with insurance companies said she had handled it. But now she was out on sick leave, and the problem grew labyrinthine in its complexity. Finally Ronnie discovered that the secretary had had a nervous breakdown. To try to resolve the problem, Ronnie enlisted Tony's support as well as that of her accountant and a lawyer.

As anyone who has had to deal with elaborate doctor's bills and insurance reimbursements knows, they are arcanely complicated, which I am certain is done on purpose. Nobody could figure out if the money had been applied to my bill or used for something else or what. It was virtually untraceable.

One night I erupted because I didn't feel well and it seemed as if the bills were a bigger issue than I was. Sometimes the bills put Tony over the edge, which I understood but still resented because usually it ended up stealing attention I needed. On this night I grabbed a stack of them from Tony and stuffed them in the toilet. I ended up drying them out on the living room floor, and Tony and I admitted to each other we had reached the breaking point on the insurance mess. What we didn't know was that another major issue was bubbling beneath the surface.

Because I had gone through over $200,000 of my insurance coverage in only a few years, a red flag had gone up and a case manager was assigned to me. At first I thought this was a bad thing, but it was not. The woman assigned to me explained in our introductory phone call that case managers were both registered nurses as well as patient advocates. If she determined that the course of treatment you were getting was the best for you despite the expense, she would make the recommendation to the insurance company that you be left alone. The case manager acknowledged there was no precedent for my situation and assured me there would be considerable flexibility. It was comforting to have somebody poring over my records and keeping track of my case and assuaging my fears about blowing through my lifetime cap of $1 million, although she did say, "I had a kidney transplant guy go through four hundred thousand dollars in one day."

Apparently, throughout the early fall the case manager had been in contact with my doctor's office about her discovery that it was charging considerably more for my treatment than comparable area facilities, such as outpatient hospital treatment centers. But she knew I was very comfortable there and tried to negotiate a better price for both my treatment and the drug. The doctor apparently was willing to throw in the chair—you pay $300 for the time you spend in the chair during each treatment—but that wasn't good enough. The case manager had discovered I could get the gamma globulin for almost $6,000 less per treatment almost anywhere else in the city. That was a considerable amount of money, especially since I had confided in the doctor my fears about running out of insurance. Over the course of one year that $6,000 each month added up to $72,000. The case manager brought all this to my attention only when she'd gotten nowhere negotiating with the doctor, who had told her, "If Bill Clinton gets elected she won't have to worry about a cap." I kind of freaked when the case manager repeated that to me, especially since I was close to my doctor. But she told me to remain calm and she'd continue to deal with it. In the meantime I was also upset about the $23,000 owed my father that nobody could seem to locate.

All of this was separate from my relationship with the doctor, which had always been excellent. Unfortunately, nothing was being discovered about my illness, and we'd fallen into too comfortable a pattern where I hardly saw the doctor but just came in for treatment. But I felt as secure as you can possibly be when you've got a serious illness and nobody knows how you got it and how to treat it long-term, and I would never have gone elsewhere if I hadn't been forced to.

While all this was going on, behind the scenes Abigail's father really pushed my father to take me to see a doctor at Memorial Sloan-Kettering Cancer Center. I was not opposed to it, but my father resisted for a lot of reasons. I got a good glimpse of the first one when I checked in at the desk in the

lobby, right next to the sign that says THE SERVICES RENDERED
IN THIS BUILDING ARE MADE POSSIBLE, IN PART, THROUGH
THE FRANK SINATRA FUND.

The man behind the computer terminal entered my name
and asked, "Which Rosemary Breslin are you?" He then
read the first of two birth dates. I interrupted: "That was my
mother. She's dead." Of course, his next question for my
personal profile was "Mother's maiden name?" It blows my
mind that insurance companies, banks and credit cards all ask
for your mother's maiden name as part of their identification
system. It really lifts my spirits to make a bank transaction and
be asked, "Mother's maiden name." Didn't anyone ever think
that each time you fill out a form it might be slightly upsetting
to have to write down the name of the person you loved the
most in the world and lost at an early age? Then again, my
mother would say, "Get past it, Rosemary. You've got bigger
things to deal with." She was not big on self-indulgence.

Though I had been there with my mother when she had a
blood transfusion, what was happening to me now never
brought back memories of what she had been through. I dealt
with that when it happened, and for my whole life will have to
bear my loss. But I know my mother would feel herself a
failure if I used what had happened to her as a crutch to
contend with my own situation.

And I had her name to live up to. My older brothers, who
are identical twins, were only twenty months old when my
mother realized she was again pregnant. Immediately after I
was born she clearly suffered a period of postpartum depression, telling my father I was not her baby and she would have
nothing to do with me. For three weeks he had to change me
and feed me, and when she still insisted I was not hers, he
had to name me. He named me after the woman he loved

most in the world. So I think my name is an honor, something clearly better than I.

So here I was, the second Rosemary Breslin in a decade hanging in the halls of Sloan-Kettering. I guess that's some kind of a legacy. Upstairs, a phlebotomist—I love that name—took blood, and we then waited to see the doctor. I had vowed this was only going to be a consultation and if they wanted any of my body parts I was out of there. Twice during the wait, my father wanted to leave. Fortunately Abigail's father stopped by to calm him down and even managed to get a monosyllabic response or two.

We finally got in to see the doctor, who had some vague but encouraging things to say, talked about research at Sloan-Kettering and presented a number of possible scenarios. I realized I needed to be doing this, that I had been too lulled in the cocoon of my own doctor's office. When this doctor suggested I have a bone marrow exam that morning and then one again immediately following treatment to see if there was any difference, I said "Yes." So much for my "nobody's touching me." But I thought they might have to get my father some smelling salts. He has such a delicate constitution. So there I was again, facedown on an examination table, one leg rhythmically kicking while some sadist stuck a huge needle into my right hipbone. And the part where a bone sample was removed sounded just like a corkscrew going through my back. "You're going to feel a lot of pressure," the woman administering the procedure warned. That's damn right, I thought. It feels as if someone stuck the needle from the Empire State Building in your back and then balanced the rest of the building's weight on you.

Actually, not only was the woman not a sadist but she was so good at the exam that it hurt the least ever, which means it was merely excruciating. In a move for sympathy I said, "I've had six others of these in the past three years." She shook her head and then said, "I have leukemia patients who get one every month." Shut me right up.

Although I was impressed with Sloan-Kettering, I was not ready to commit to a move here. But I was willing to see this new doctor in addition to my own.

Soon after, the move made itself. The insurance company started paying only the portion of my treatment bill that was the same amount as the most expensive alternative the case manager could find in New York. In less than two months, my uncovered portion was over $12,000. In addition, my stepmother, Tony, an accountant and a lawyer had finally been able to get to the root of the problem with the missing reimbursement check. In fact, it didn't exist because the secretary at the doctor's office who had had a nervous breakdown, and who had yet to return, never resubmitted my insurance forms and far longer than the year deadline had passed. The result was that Ronnie and my father were out the $23,000.

All this confusion about money may sound as if we were not on top of things. But we were. It's simply impossible for anyone to keep all this in order unless you devote your entire life to it. For example, my insurance company had always paid 100 percent of the gamma globulin treatments, so why would I have suspected I was being ridiculously overcharged. What should I have done? Called area institutions and asked what they charge? In retrospect, the answer might be yes. But I was unaware there was a problem and my medical situation already took up so much of my time that I resisted devoting more to it. Also, the people surrounding me—my father, Ronnie and Tony—all had full-time jobs. I felt guilty about it because I had three intelligent, motivated people devoting too much time to this already. And still they couldn't get it straightened out. A father had a sick child and he was contacting doctors throughout the world to see if anyone could help. Should he have given less time to that and more to analyzing the bills? And my stepmother had to take care of him when the whole situation got to be too much, something nobody would ever tell me, but it's pretty easy to figure out. And my husband, whose main job was bolstering me when it all came crashing down, could hardly take on any more.

So I was burdened by tremendous guilt about the time and money my illness was stealing from other people. But I couldn't take on more guilt because then this illness would steal my whole life. And, at all times I asked myself, How long is your whole life?

The Winter of My Discontent

All of this was happening in the winter of 1993, which was progressing quite miserably for me. Not my home life—the only thing that truly mattered—but everything else. At home I was perfecting my Donna Reed. Tony was on a real roll with work. Right after finishing the film in which Lena Olin chops off her arm, he went to work on Arnold Schwarzenegger's *Last Action Hero*. The job, unlike the released film, went extremely well, except for one major glitch, which was beyond Tony's control, but he actually solved the problem quite deftly. In the movie a huge balloon of Arnold was supposed to loom over Times Square. But when the head was finally blown up in Tony's shop it looked nothing like Schwarzenegger. This was on a Saturday and the balloon was to go up the next day. Tony called me at home, and I called Kevin, who called a friend who made costumes for *One Life to Live,* and she brought over her sewing machine while scenic artists, using a photo of Arnold, repainted the face so it bore some resemblance to him while the seamstress cut and sewed different parts of the head, which were not in proportion to the body.

This was all on the weekend the World Trade Center was bombed. The bomb had gone off on Friday morning, and all that day black smoke could be seen from our corner.

New York was not exactly in an easygoing mood when I picked up Tony from work on Monday in Times Square. High in the sky above was the sixty-foot balloon of Arnold with a shotgun in one hand and dynamite in the other. On the car ride home, I asked Tony if anybody had thought it was bad timing for Arnold to be holding dynamite. He said he'd already thought the same thing, but hated this balloon so much that he said nothing. That night, when I mentioned the dynamite to my father, he thought it was one of the most irresponsible things he'd ever heard of.

By 10 P.M. our phone was ringing. The mayor, the governor and most of the city of New York wanted the balloon down. It was all over the news. I, of course, had to antagonize Tony by laughing the entire time he tried to solve the problem. In the meantime the woman from the balloon company had chosen this time to have a nervous breakdown and disappear. Maybe she was with the secretary from my doctor's office. Finally, the balloon was deflated, and in the huge, vacant space of the old Nathan's in Times Square Arnold was laid out, and with some quick artistry they removed the badge from his belt buckle and put it in his hand. So now he was holding a gun in one hand and the badge in the other, which apparently was acceptable.

For some reason vacuuming, watching the soaps, planning meals and going to the gym along with my hospital duty, were just not doing it anymore. I really thought I had made the desire to work disappear, but I hadn't. What was it with me, why was I no longer living up to the name I'd chosen for myself. Deadbeat. And, as Ken Cole pointed out, nobody did it better than I. Part of the new me was a strong belief in doing all things well, and as a deadbeat I was nonpareil. But at the worst of times, my middle-class nature sneaks through.

However, my desire to write and somebody wanting to hire me to do so were two completely different stories. Nobody wanted me. An editor I worked for at the *Daily News* called me about a job at *People* magazine. Now, I may not be the best or the brightest, but I felt it was a job I could handle. Yet before I even sat down in the editor's office, she said, "I've been thinking about it and I don't know if you're right for the job." I remember saying to myself, "It would have been nice if you'd thought of that before you called me." Of course, she hadn't seen or spoken to me in five years, and I guess it didn't seem possible that I might have grown up a bit in that time. But after thirty seconds with me she should have seen that I was pretty solid. I had no intention of mentioning my illness; no one needed to know that I had had to have my whole life collapse for me to get it together. The editor mentioned I had been a "little flighty" when I worked for her. I wanted to say that if I were ever to hire someone from the ages of twenty-five to twenty-eight, "a little flighty" would be a prerequisite because otherwise you get these slightly robotic journalists who can put a sentence together but bring nothing of interest in their own lives to the table. Anyway, that's my opinion, but it is right.

The editor at *People* then mentioned maybe I'd be good for the special issues they put together when people like Audrey Hepburn and Jackie O. die and the articles are extended photo captions. I was supposed to send copies of some of my old stories to some guy, but I left and decided not to bother.

To be turned down by *People* when they'd called you. I was definitely working my way down the food chain.

Around this time, a friend sent me a package in the mail. A few months before I met Tony I'd been in the running for the job of ghostwriting Dawn Steel's book, her own tales from the front. I'd met with Dawn at her office on Dopey Drive or one of those other Disney streets. She opened the meeting by saying, "I hear we have a good friend in common." When she said the woman's name, my heart sank. She named someone I loved dearly but who no longer spoke to me. I didn't mention this to Dawn. After all, what could I say, "Oh, Margo. I'm not exactly her favorite person."

Anyway, after discussing her objectives for about forty-five minutes, Dawn made it clear I was "a long shot" for the job because she was looking for somebody with experiences closer to her own, someone a little older, more familiar with Dawn's struggle to raise a child while grappling with an intense and high-profile position. I offered that I thought the writer's job was to interpret, not mirror someone else's life, but she hired someone else anyway. That blow hurt a little, but what really killed what little ego I had left was that when the book appeared right after I'd been rejected by *People*, I saw that it was written somewhere around the fourth-grade level. To be passed over hurts no matter who you are, but to have an illiterate chosen over you can really hurt. But the worst was yet to come.

This midget real estate mogul, Mort Zuckerman, had purchased the *Daily News* and was weeding out a lot of the old rot, of which there was plenty, and bringing in some fresh talent. Although I had been "a little flighty" when I worked at the *News*, I had proved myself to be one of the better writers there. Now I was not only five years older, but also had the calm and secure Tony behind me and I knew it could bring a new quality to my work. I submitted to Mort two pieces I'd taken great care in writing, but heard nothing. I figured Hey, it happens, and each time I walked past the McDonald's on Sixth Avenue with the HELP WANTED sign in the window, I felt tempted. Then, what should come in the mail but a form rejection letter that looked as if it had been run off a mimeograph machine that class exams were produced on in the early sixties. To not even be considered for a job at a place where I had done fairly well before was pretty much my low point. In my note to Mort I had even said I was willing to work on a freelance basis, but obviously I wasn't good enough even for that.

When I opened the form rejection letter I experienced the purest form of humiliation I have ever known. I threw it away without telling Tony or anyone else about it. I wish I had saved it. Not because I now think of myself as such a success, but because I think it's really funny, especially when I try to read the *News* and would rate the writing just a tad beneath the level of that in Dawn's book. But in the months that followed, I experienced a dull pain each time I read the *News* and saw the byline of some new talentless wannabe.

Of course, it didn't help that at all times my father was screaming in the background, "What are you doing with your life?" Then Tony, who was unaware of the extent to which I'd been rejected, said, "Why don't you just write. Who cares if it gets published. I think you'll be a lot happier."

Maybe I would have been, because, oddly enough, though nobody wanted to hire me, I didn't question myself. Probably because I'm an idiot. But for the first time ever, I didn't let these humiliations tear at my center. I knew that all my Susie Homemaking and my total absorption in Tony Dunne's life were teaching me something. I still didn't know what it was, but I knew it was important, and even if I couldn't seem to figure it out or use it for anything now, I knew I was going to. I suspected I was doing some kind of research, but what kind was the real mystery. Maybe my greatest work was to be the woman behind the man, which I had no trouble with, but definitely would drive my father out of his mind. Tony says my father pushes me so hard because he believes so strongly in my talent. I contend it's because he's a pain who has an insatiable need to meddle.

So with no job prospects in my future, I turned back to domesticity. And, unfortunately, all was not quiet on the medical front, which was taking up more and more of my time.

I had made the transition to being treated at Sloan-Kettering quite smoothly, mostly because the nurses there were just as nurturing as the ones at the doctor's office. They made me feel very secure. At Sloan, I had a plusher deal than at the doctor's office. The Adult Day Hospital is on the seventeenth floor with sweeping views of the East River, and most times I had a room with a bed, TV and two chairs. But it was still a new environment to me, and it was a hospital, a cancer hospital. I like to joke that I should open the baseball cap and scarf concession in the lobby, right next to the Frank Sinatra sign. Maybe he'd want to get in on it with some signature hairpieces. We could make a bundle.

The most notable difference from the protected world of a small Upper East Side doctor's office and Sloan-Kettering was the clientele. Most of them were significantly sicker than the crowd at the doctor's office. Though most of the patients were a great deal older than I, because of the sheer volume I met a lot more people closer to my own age. You would think that being the healthiest person in a crowd would make you feel better, but for me this was the most difficult part of the transition.

On one of my first visits to Sloan-Kettering, my roommate was a thirty-year-old guy who on his first wedding anniversary found out that he had inoperable lung cancer. On this day the treatment had made him so sick he didn't want to continue with it. And the doctors told him it wasn't working. After he left, my nurse, in a rare display of savage frustration, said, "I wanted to tell him that's right, just forget it, go live your life. This isn't worth it. But I couldn't."

There was also a younger woman with the most luxuriant red hair. I'd seen her at the doctor's clinic downstairs, and she looked pretty good. It was only when I spotted the red hair lying on the table beside her bed that I realized she was the pale, gray, bald woman sharing the room with me. And trust me, I am a champion wig spotter. In my first few months at Sloan-Kettering, I watched her go from being agile to walking so slowly that you could see the actual movement in her hips.

Both she and the lung cancer guy disappeared from the scene pretty quickly. I felt more vulnerable and much more frightened that this someday might be me. Also, during my first few months at Sloan-Kettering the gamma globulin was proving to be increasingly ineffective. Until then, it had brought my blood count up to the normal range. Now it was barely getting me out of the basement and was lasting for shorter and shorter periods of time. In a span of three months I dropped from every twenty-eight days to more like eighteen or nineteen, and with barely perceptible results. For one of the first times since it all started, I felt like a sick person. Lots of times I could walk only a few blocks, and if I went up a flight of stairs my heart began pounding. Besides the physical effects, the mental ones were pretty bad. First of all, I was terrified of what was happening to me and I dealt with it by either keeping it completely inside, clinging to Tony or taking it all out on him. I said this was happening because "they" made me leave my doctor and come to this place where everybody dies. The real story was that my body had gotten too used to the gamma globulin, and the antibody, no longer affected by it, was killing off my red blood cells almost as rapidly as I was making them.

At home, I had this real fantasy life of newlywed bliss, married less than a year and more deeply in love by the day, and yet it felt as if it were all slipping away. At exactly the same time Tony got a big job on the movie *The Paper*, which was going to take almost all his time and concentration for the next eight months. It was important for me not to cave in completely to fear. You can't ask someone to work incredibly hard so they can be extremely successful and then whine, "What about me?"

Whenever I did whine, Tony would say, "I saved you from a fate on Roosevelt Island," where my father's sister Deirdre lived. "You'd be living in the second bedroom and wearing a stained sweatsuit and Ronnie would be paying Dee to handle you and you'd get a small allowance which you'd spend on Entenmann's and vodka, so you'd weigh about two hundred pounds. And you would do nothing all day."

"Tell me more. Tell me more," I'd beg, and he would go into further detail. When I repeated the story to my stepmother, there was a hollow ring to her laugh.

And Tony was doing everything he could for me, but often I was asking the impossible. I didn't want to be sick. It's that simple. Except that being sick was now a big part of me and of the person I had become. It had moved from being this external thing that had happened to me and might go away or might kill me to this huge part of my life I may have to live with. As I looked around me, the more I understood how lucky I was to have this option. When my new doctor scratched his head as he tried to figure out how else to treat me, since the gamma globulin wasn't working, I refused to fall apart. And when he decided to supplement my gamma diet with a side order of red blood cells, I only freaked mildly. Gamma globulin is a nice, clear, benign-looking substance, whereas the red bags of blood are ominous-looking. Also, gamma globulin has no side effects, but blood comes with a bunch of them. Forget AIDS, there're several varieties of hepatitis, iron buildup, screwing up your bones and at least twenty-six other possibilities, yours for the offering. Everyone assures you these are all rare occurrences, but when it's your life, rare is rarely rare enough.

The most significant difference between the gamma globu-lin and blood transfusions is that when the former is effective, my body actually works on its own and makes my own blood, whereas the latter just dumps the blood in my system and I use it up until I need more—I don't make any myself. Be-cause this is the case, from the moment I get the blood I'm using it up, so I'm on my way down right from the beginning. This plays games with your head more than your body. Also, the blood transfusions only brought my counts up to the very bottom of the normal range, which meant I was fairly lethar-gic. A blood transfusion lasts for a maximum of two weeks, so between stopping in to get my blood counts—the three days a month for the gamma globulin and the two days each month for blood—I was spending an inordinate amount of time at the hospital.

One day that has stayed with me was a Friday when the junior membership took over the infusion room. There was a twenty-eight-year-old woman getting platelets because her first bone marrow transplant had failed. She was in a little bit of a hurry because she had a 4 P.M. nail appointment so that she would look perfect in the black velvet dress she would wear to her sister's wedding the next night. As I went to answer a phone call in the hall, wheeling my pole along with me, I saw her father crumpled against the wall. He smelled of alcohol, and I later overheard a doctor say the father had held up well, but had now started to drink because he knew there wasn't going to be a second attempt at a second bone marrow transplant but couldn't bring himself to tell his daughter. He also probably suspected that the daughter knew. Every sick person I've met has instinctively known what's going on without being told.

Diagonally across from me sat a young woman who snuggled with her twenty-three-year-old boyfriend as if they were hanging in his living room, not at a hospital where he was receiving chemotherapy. A pale blue bandanna covered his head, which he had chosen to shave rather than wait for his hair to fall out. Among the three of us in the room, we had eighty-seven years, not enough to rate a "Happy Birthday" from Willard Scott.

The other daughter and I were there with our fathers, and the son was with both his parents. All the parents eyed each other and eyed our Naugahyde chairs thinking that if they could just jump in them the situation would be reversed. And the children all looked at one another with eyes that read, Here we are, sick, and still the worst thing about it is the guilt you feel about doing this to your parents. It was one of the few times my father couldn't mask his sheer horror of the situation. When I was finished, he ran for the elevator. And I, the old lady of the bunch, having turned thirty-six a few days before,

went home that night and cried to Tony that I was scared and
didn't want to die. To get me to stop, Tony agreed to do his
impression of Dustin Hoffman in *Rain Man.* Laughing
through the tears, I said, "I'm worried. You do it too good."
Other times I would make him play multiple-personality
Tony, where he'd pull different characters out of his head and
make them perform for me.

Tony was great about entertaining me after he had finished
a fifteen-hour day and had another one ahead of him. He was
getting good at knowing those times when I'd reached my
breaking point, which were usually exhibited when I was lying
in bed, my head propped on the pillow with tears streaming
down my face. I figured the least I could do was make it
straightforward for him.

One night, one of my worst, when I felt depressed and
tired of the whole situation, just to name a few of my feelings,
Tony turned to me with tears in his eyes and said, "I wish I
were the sick one."

"Oh, no," I said in a terrified tone. "If we counted on me
earning a living, we'd be destitute. You have to be the healthy
one. You have to bring home the bacon."

And we were starting to see the tangible results of Tony's
efforts to find work. The phone rang frequently and he now
had his choice of jobs. It's a lot of fun to be around someone
who loves what he does and excells at it. Sort of like watching
me with a vacuum cleaner. I remember visiting Tony when he
was constructing the main set of *The Paper,* the newsroom,
out of a raw space. He instructed a crew of maybe forty men
while he and the art director tried to resolve a problem with
one of the drawings. I could tell there was order in the apparent chaos and a thrill in the tension of trying to figure out how
to make something that worked on paper work in real life.

Certain sets are extremely complicated. I know because I make Tony explain them to me fifty times.

With Tony happily booked on his job until late October and my health generally sucking, the summer following the one in which we were married was not a lot of fun for me. To almost everyone I looked fine, but normal activities like swimming and biking were now tests of endurance. And since I have always staved off most of my anxieties through athletics, I wasn't a whole lot of fun to be around.

Because my doctor thought gamma globulin and blood transfusions weren't enough, he decided to try a drug called Epogen, which stimulates red blood cell growth. He was fairly sure it wouldn't work because I was making plenty of red blood cells on my own; the problem was they were just being killed off. But he and other specialists felt it was worth the try because maybe I'd make more than I needed and more would survive the attack.

"You'll have to administer it three times a week subcutaneously," he said as he wrote the prescription.

"What's that?" I asked of that last word.

"Beneath the skin."

"Huh?"

"You inject it. You take a half-hour class," he said.

"Oh," I said, but thought, Shoot me. Just get it over with and shoot me.

I was on the verge of tears throughout the whole class where we learned to inject ourselves, and only restrained myself from out-and-out hysteria when the woman next to me blithely jabbed the syringe into her thigh and told me, "I'm learning this because I'm going to inject my mother." She had the needle in and out in five seconds. The nurse had to put her hand on me to get me to do it.

At home it was no better. I would make ten false attempts
at stabbing it into my fat thigh, but couldn't do it. Finally,
Tony said, "Let me do it."

"What?"

"Well, now it's part of your illness that we can share."

This guy is out of his mind, I thought.

It became our three-times-a-week routine. I'd get the syringe ready and sterilize the area, and he'd stick it in. I figured
he loved me more than I could ever have imagined because I
wouldn't list my upper thighs as one of the wonders of the
modern world.

But I wish my doctor had told me who else uses this drug.
Usually I scrutinize the folded-up piece of paper about a drug
because it can tell you a lot, but this time I only glanced at it.
So I ran around telling all these people about trying the drug
and someone said to me, "Oh yeah, they give that to a lot of
people with AIDS." Which means all the people who suspect
I'm not being straightforward about my illness and are certain
I really have AIDS will now be convinced I have it. I don't
have a problem with AIDS, just as I don't have one with
cancer—except that I don't want either one—but neither is
what I have. I'm a little territorial about my illness.

The doctor said it would be a minimum of six weeks to
about three months before we knew if the drug was working or
not. It had no side effects and I never even felt the needles,
but I didn't try to inject myself because I liked Tony's having
to do it.

Though I thought I'd given up my professional life, in the
shower one morning I figured out what I had been up to and
what I wanted to do. It came to me as I was working up a
good lather with the shampoo. Maybe I had stimulated the
few brain cells left. I decided I couldn't handle more rejection,

so I called up someone who believed in my talent, someone who had hired me as a copy boy on the lobster shift when I was seventeen, my friend Don Forst, then the editor of New York *Newsday* and told him I wanted to write about being sick. I gave him two or three succinct sentences on the phone, and he said to come in that morning. I knew I was on to something. It really did come together just like that. All of a sudden, these last three years of not working at all were really ones of gathering information, distancing myself from it and interpreting it.

At *Newsday*, I met with Don and an editor, Stanley Mieses. I recognized Stanley because, twelve years before, he had tried to date me and I hadn't returned his phone calls. As I spoke with them about writing a series of articles, I could tell they got it and knew I could offer a pretty comprehensive and unique view of being ill—hospitals, insurance, doctors, all the things I'd been around these past four years and stored away. We didn't really get into it deeply, and Stanley and I immediately clicked. Before I left, Stanley said, "I think we know each other."

"Ah, yeah," I said.

"I think you blew me off."

"It was actually a compliment," I replied. "You weren't enough of a jerk for me to go out with you."

I left elated. Suddenly, I had a job. It wasn't a big one, but it was a great one. And it was one I was uniquely qualified to do. Tony was thrilled without being patronizing. It was evident he had tremendous faith in my abilities even though in all our time together I had barely put a single word on paper.

At the same time *Newsday* hired me the only other beacon of good fortune shone my way. It was late October, and Tony had a few weeks off after he finished *The Paper* and before he began work on a Nora Ephron movie. I said I wanted to go on a road trip. My nurses, Elizabeth Halton and Ann Culkin, sensing my desperate need for a little normalcy, persuaded my doctor to let them pump me up with gamma globulin and a few pints of blood so I could disappear for a few weeks. We left the city on a dark rainy afternoon.

On our first day I was standing in front of a country inn in Virginia. A carload of four old ladies were dropped off at the curb. They had two canes, one walker and over three hundred years among them. On the small step leading to the inn's heavy front door, the first woman teetered back and forth precariously, so I ran over and held open the door until the last woman with the walker made it through.

"Thank you," she said.

"No problem," I replied.

"Wish I had none," she said as she shuffled along and smiled at me, the picture of health, my cheeks still rosy from a tough morning bike ride.

I hesitated and then answered lightly, "Me too."

For me to take this trip, I'd had two separate transfusions of two pints of red blood cells and six half-gallons of intravenous gamma globulin over a three-day period. In my bag were a six-pack of syringes for the road and a twelve-pack of the drug that we were pretty sure wasn't working but my doctor wanted to give a few more weeks just in case. In my wallet I made sure I carried my red Patient Medical Alert Card that says I have an implanted PORT-A-CATH access device, and I reminded Tony that in an emergency I needed irradiated red blood cells. None of the plain old stuff for me. And the old lady had looked at me with envy.

But I felt great, something I hadn't felt for nearly nine months. Tony and I roamed the back roads of Virginia, and I babbled about every subject on earth and got Tony to tell me stories of growing up and work and school and whatever.

We stopped in at the Homestead in Virginia, where the spa is original, over one hundred years old, and they've got these white tile rooms with bathtubs in the middle of them; you're supposed to get in and sit in the dark, and the bathtub just keeps overflowing and afterward you walk over and stand in front of high-powered shower heads. As I approached the room next to Tony's I balked. "No way. This is some kind of Gestapo treatment. When I think 'spa' I think something like Canyon Ranch, not some weirdo torture chamber. If I go in there, I'm never comin' out." I then ran away to the safety of the rocking chairs on the huge veranda.

"You should have done it," Tony said when he found me. "It felt unbelievably good."

"You want to get rid of me."

We then drove down the Shenandoah Highway at the height of the autumn foliage. We stopped for sodas in a backwater town, and on the checkout counter was a large bowl with a face plastered on it and a hand-printed plea for money to help pay for a young boy's bone marrow transplant.

Next we cut across the state of North Carolina and took a small ferry to a windswept island off the Outer Banks called Ocracoke. Just the name brings peace to my soul. I'd read about it somewhere, called the Chamber of Commerce and got the name of a real estate agent who rented us a house with sweeping views of Pamlico Sound. In the early mornings the only activities outside our windows were the small fishing boats heading out and, in the sky above, migrating Canadian geese. The first morning I woke up and watched thousands of them fly by the bedroom window in perfect military formation.

All the tourists were gone, so, except for the fishermen, we had the island almost completely to ourselves. I was so grateful to feel like a regular person and was so into hanging out with Tony, I would follow him into the bathroom until he took to locking me out.

Every day we took a twenty-mile bike ride along the flat national seashore, a ten-mile stretch with no houses on it. I'm usually the rah-rah group leader when it comes to getting Tony to exercise, but I was pumping as hard as I could and I couldn't keep up with him, so every few miles he'd stop and look back over his shoulder and watch the little figure chugging along until I came into closer view. When I'd reach him, I'd be beaming, but wouldn't stop pedaling because it would be too hard to stop. One night Tony turned to me, in one of the rare times I've seen him close to tears, and confessed, "When I look back and see you so far behind and trying so hard, it just breaks my heart."

"Don't think of it like that," I replied. "I'm just having the greatest time. I'm like the little engine that could." But for the rest of the week I'd catch that look in his eyes when I caught up to him on the deserted road. All I could say was "But I'm having the time of my life," which I think broke his heart even more.

At the end of most days we'd stop over at the piers and buy fresh fish, shrimp and clams for dinner, and we'd eat while watching spectacular sunsets from our porch. It's all true. I couldn't make this stuff up.

The master bedroom suite's bathroom had double everything, including a double Jacuzzi with a picture window on the water. I would soak in there before dinner, but couldn't get Mr. Romance into the tub with me. Otherwise, I'd say our trip qualifies as a key montage in the goyim version of a Barbra Streisand movie.

It was here on Ocracoke in the early morning, while Tony slept upstairs, that I sat down at the dining room table overlooking the still waters of the sound and started to write again. Just days before we left New York, though I'd never told either Ronnie or my father about writing the series for *Newsday*, Ronnie had asked, "Would you like a laptop?"

"I would love one." I had to have the first piece finished by the time we got back and had been bummed at the thought of lugging my big old computer with us.

Now I sat at this table in front of a brand-new PowerBook and began writing my tales from the front for the newspaper with the door opening out onto the screened porch, and it felt great. From the very first words I typed, I knew the writer who returned to her work was very different from the one who had stopped. I intuitively understood that my work and I are one and the same, and I had reached a point where the two were perfectly integrated. Once in my life, off the coast of Maine, I dived off a high rock and from the moment my toes pushed off from the boulder it felt perfect. I sliced through the water with a feeling I'll never have again. That feeling I now got from the writing I had so aggressively stayed away from. I have to believe a part of me knew what it was doing, knew when to stop and when to go back.

When we returned to New York, Tony started work on the Nora Ephron movie *Mixed Nuts*. Fortunately, Tony already had the job when my stepmother blocked Nora Ephron's path in the aisle at Fairway and said, "I hope you're going to hire my son-in-law."

"I can get my jobs myself," Tony later said, but clearly didn't mind that Ronnie was in there pitching for him.

"Yeah, well, my family believes in dispensing with the subtleties and just making sure the deal is set."

My first piece ran in *Newsday* on the first Wednesday in November, and it was immediately successful. I wrote an article every two weeks and spent a lot of time on each one. And I was getting paid. It was a small amount, but for two solid years I had earned zero, so $1,200 for the first piece and $400 for each subsequent one was big bucks for me. Of course, there was a dilemma.

I still had roughly $13,000 in debts, none of which I had told Tony about. My first $2,000 went to paying off the IRS and then one of three friends who had helped me out. I determined that I would pay back each debt in the order I had borrowed the money. Tony casually asked me what I was doing with my money, and I would shrug and laugh and I hated that I had to make it seem as if I were being completely frivolous with it, when really I wasn't spending a penny and was even diverting a little extra from the household money.

On the Wednesday before Thanksgiving the phone started to ring, all my friends in Los Angeles reporting that my first piece had been reprinted on the cover of the *Los Angeles Times*'s view section. It was a good ego boost and I got to brag a little to Tony.

On Friday morning a clerk from the *Times* called and asked if he could give Frank Zappa my phone number. Frank had called and asked for it. Oh no, don't give Frank Zappa, who is on his deathbed, my number. He had advanced prostate cancer, and just a few months before, he'd had an orchestral piece premiere at Lincoln Center's Avery Fisher Hall; when he didn't attend I knew only one thing could have stopped him. Frank died before he got a chance to call me, but I really believe it's as if we did have a conversation. Other people say, "It's too bad you didn't get a chance to talk to him," but I know better.

Later that day, around four o'clock, I sat in the semidark of the living room, curled up in a big leather chair, when the phone rang. The voice on the other end introduced himself as David Milch, creator and producer with Stephen Bochco of one of the hottest new shows on television, *N.Y.P.D. Blue*.

"I read your story and I think you could write for us. You seem to have the right sensibility. Are you familiar with our show?"

"Yes."

"Would you like to write an episode of the show?"

"Yes."

"I'll send you all the scripts and tapes we've got and take your time and then start to think of some ideas. Call me whenever you think you're ready." He then gave me both his work and home numbers.

"Okay. Thank you very much."

"I'm delighted," David Milch said.

I hung up the phone. This guy is out of his mind, I thought. He's got the best show on television and he's "delighted" I'm willing to write for him. Think back. It was exactly one year ago that the midget real estate mogul had sent me the form rejection letter, and now the most-talked-about television show in the nation, one singled out for the quality of its writing, wanted to hire me. I did a little strutting around the house that weekend. Tony was in a slight state of shock. "I never doubted what you were capable of," he said. He was the one who had nurtured me back to the point where I could work. "But I never thought things would happen this fast."

Life was as perfect as it could get except for my health. The gamma globulin had stopped working. Tony was still shooting me up, but we were pretty sure it wasn't doing much.

I was getting two units of red blood cells every ten days or so, and that was keeping me among the living. I couldn't stand the cold outside and would shiver for a long time after I went out no matter how warmly I dressed, and I'm somebody who used to need only a thick sweater in the dead of winter. And I got this stupid little cough. It was one of those little tics that made you want to clear your throat all the time. I mentioned it to my doctor and he sent me for a chest X ray, but nothing showed up. He said it was probably related to my low blood count. I had had coughs before when I was low because it's hard to breathe, but as week after week wore on, I said, "This feels different." But nothing showed up on any blood tests. Sometimes I ran a low-grade fever, but I had done that before as well. The whole winter I never felt well and would say to Tony, "In a whole year, the only time I felt well was in Ocracoke." Mostly, I left the house only to get blood transfusions, as I watched blizzard after blizzard hit New York from my spot beneath the down comforter.

During this time, I kept myself isolated from all other patients at the hospital. I didn't want to see or speak with anyone. It took too much effort, and most times I was on the verge of tears because I was so scared about what was happening to me. I dragged myself out of bed to get my transfusions and dragged myself home afterward, and that was my life. One time, while sitting at the foot of the bed, my father started a conversation with an old woman patient and her friend. They had been having a long talk about whether the woman's friend should have taken the roast out of the oven before she came to the hospital. Then they debated watching *Matlock*.

"I've seen them all," the friend said. "But I love that Andy Griffith."

"Where are you from?" my father asked.

"Woodlawn," the old lady answered, referring to a once all Irish section of the Bronx. "You know it?"

"Sure, I know it," my father said. "How is it?"

"Oh, it's still very nice," the other replied. She then paused. "You know. No teddy bears there."

"Excuse me?"

"You know what I'm talking about," she said firmly. "No teddy bears there."

My father, at first confused, started to shake with laughter. I held my hand over my mouth to silence my laughter. Neither of us had ever heard anyone call blacks teddy bears, and we knew it was wrong, but the old lady was just too funny. It was the first time in months I had done anything but lie there listlessly. All my nurses were concerned, but were assured by my doctor that my lack of energy was the combination of my weakened condition and the bitter cold. Still, by February the little tickle at the base of my throat had become a hacking cough, but tests continued to show nothing.

Fortunately, I got a gift from God in the form of an extended trip to L.A. The latter part of Tony's movie was going to be filmed in California, and from March through May we would be staying at a new hotel on the beach in Santa Monica.

This fit perfectly with David Milch's *N.Y.P.D. Blue* schedule. We would go over my ideas and I could start work in March, and he'd be finished with the bulk of his work for first season by early April and would then help me as much as I needed. I was smart enough to know that forty-six minutes of television may not seem like a lot, but it is. So now, in addition to writing my columns for *Newsday* I spent my days poring over murder stories in the newspaper, always one of my favorite activities.

When I was six, all the kids in my class wrote little books on construction paper and bound them with fuzzy ribbons. I was giving mine to my grandmother, who had bragged to all her friends about my artistic abilities. The book was written in pencil on orange paper. I had forgotten about it, but my grandmother showed it to me when I was in my early twenties. "I was so embarrassed," she said. "I told all my friends I'd show it to them. They all had pretty drawings from their grandchildren." My book had three stories. The first one involved a robbery at Alexander's on Queens Boulevard. The security guard shot and killed the thief as he ran from the store. I had a little pencil drawing of the scene opposite the text. My next story involved the theft of a case of Coke from a candy store. The owner shot and killed the thief, and I had the splattered bottles on the sidewalk in front of the body. The last story involved another robbery—only this time the suspect was shot but not killed. Even at that age I understood the need to mix it up a bit. Instead of showing the book to her friends, my grandmother hid it in a drawer and paid a visit to Saint Pancras Church off Myrtle Avenue in Glendale, Queens, and put in a pitch for me. She wasn't all that religious, but recognized a soul in need when she saw one. Much as I loved Mary Poppins, I had also seen *The Bad Seed* on the Million Dollar Movie after school and gotten a little rush from it. A little girl who killed people.

From the *Newsday* computer bank I got several years' worth of stories on what I deemed interesting crimes and murders for my episode of *N.Y.P.D. Blue.*

The winter only got more brutal and I yearned to leave for L.A., convinced that I'd feel better in a warmer climate. And until we left, I was making a good dent in the blood supply in New York. My father called me Morticia. I found myself thinking about blood a good deal of the time.

With my birthday only a month away, Tony asked me what I wanted. I thought I wanted a Giorgio Armani suit. I have always wanted one and I was certain the words would flow effortlessly out of my mouth. I was already on my way to the store.

"I want you to donate blood," some other person answered. Who was this person? Not me. I wanted a Giorgio Armani suit. "I want you and all my friends to donate blood for my birthday," this space invader who had taken over my body continued.

Shut up already, I wanted to tell this alien. You're robbing me of my Giorgio Armani suit. I'd been through a lot lately and I wanted this suit, and none of that Emporio junk.

"Donate blood? That's not a present," Tony responded.

"It is for me," the invader answered.

I gave up. The suit was history. It's a sad fact that lurking somewhere inside my greedy exterior is a decent human being. I even wrote a story about it and asked people to donate blood. Finally, it was time to go to L.A. I arranged to meet David Milch in the Bochco building on the Twentieth Century–Fox lot on a Friday in March. Tony would arrive that afternoon.

The day before I left I went to the hospital for blood. I still had my hacking cough, and I said I was nervous about it. The doctor ordered a blood culture and sent me for another chest X ray. Later, when he visited me in my room on the seventeenth floor, I was hardly holding it together. I was completely worn-out and craved the curative powers of the Southern California sun.

Somehow the conversation turned to my fear of dying.

"Why are you always so afraid of dying?" the doctor asked.

I didn't know what to say. But I blurted out, with tears

falling, "Because I like my life. I just got married a little over a year ago and I'd like to have a little more time with Tony." What was I supposed to say?

When the doctor left, my nurse turned to me and said, "Was what he asked the weirdest thing you ever heard?"

"Yeah," I said. But we both understood that my doctor was assuring me I wasn't dying. Many times he had told me my illness wasn't fatal, and he was trying to say that now. He didn't mean it to sound the way it did, but he could have done a better job. And the way I was feeling made me think I had good cause to worry about dying because this sure didn't feel like living.

One thing I'd never mentioned to anyone was the chest X ray. My nurse looked at it and said maybe she saw something shadowy in the bottom of one lung but wasn't an expert at this. When the doctor later looked at it, he said it was completely clear. That's what I wanted to hear.

Welcome to L.A.

I set off the next morning for L.A. with a full supply of lemon Ricolas, which kept me from coughing continuously. This was on a Tuesday. During the plane ride thoughts of an all-expenses-paid ten-week stay at a luxury hotel by the sea filled my head. Over two months of not changing sheets or washing towels or cooking dinner or cleaning the dishes or scrubbing the toilet. And I'd be spending my time hanging out on a movie lot with the hot set.

As a treat, Tony had rented me the coolest little Mustang convertible, so I bopped around L.A. for a few days even though I felt pretty bad. But the air was warm and I convinced myself I would get better. On Friday morning I drove over to the Fox lot. I met with David Milch and gave him a few murder story lines. He picked two and told me to develop them. He introduced me around, and then we walked over to the set where he had to work on some line changes for an episode they were filming, one of the season's last.

I hung back by one of the food tables. It was a darkened

space, and in the center of it appeared a pale, thin figure perfectly lit by a single light, or so it appeared. He turned to me. "How did two kids from Queens end up in Hollywood?" David Caruso said and gave me a big hug.

"I have no idea," I replied and gave him a kiss.

I had maybe mentioned to David Milch that I knew David Caruso, but in general had kept it pretty quiet. I wanted to keep things focused on the script. But I'd known David Caruso since I first moved to Forest Hills Gardens when I was six. He was my twin brothers' age and his sister Joyce was mine. Joyce and I took ballroom dancing together, and a small group of us had loose attachments through the years.

At this time I was still unaware of the strained relations between David Caruso and the producers. After all, I'd been there for only forty-five minutes. It took me a little more than an hour to figure it out, so it probably turned out for the best that I hadn't bragged about being friends with him.

After a few hours, David Milch and I agreed that over the next few weeks I would develop my ideas and we'd get together again. Elated, I whisked down Pico Boulevard to meet Tony at the hotel.

The hotel. Shutters on the Beach. We had a seventh-floor room with a view of the Pacific. The bed had Frette sheets and the large bathroom had curtained windows that opened onto the bedroom. I hadn't seen Tony for three nights, the longest time we'd been separated in over two years. We hung out and ordered room service, and he asked me how I'd been feeling. The cough was bad, but I did feel better. Plus I'd had a fairly heady day.

On Monday morning Tony and I went to meet Dr. Melani Shaum, who was going to oversee me while I was in L.A. She asked me about the cough, which had gotten much worse over the weekend, and I briefly filled her in. She took some blood and said she'd call later with a prescription for antibiotics. She asked if my doctor in New York had mentioned trying antibiotics just to see if they would get rid of the cough. I said no.

Tony didn't have work that day, so afterward I took him for a short spin up the coast in my groovin' convertible. I tried to convince myself I was feeling OK, but after an hour I told Tony I was fading. By the time we got back to the hotel there were six or seven urgent messages from the doctor in L.A., my doctor in New York, my father, two of my nurses and several repeats. Tony called the doctor's office, and when he hung up he said, "You have to go to the hospital right now. It's very serious. The blood tests came back positive for some aggressive bacteria."

I sat on the bed caressing the Frette duvet cover, and I asked plaintively, "Can't they do something else? Can't they treat me here? I don't want to go to the hospital. Please don't make me go to the hospital." I was so weak and scared, I couldn't move. Tony called the doctor back, but she insisted and said she would meet us at UCLA Medical Center.

By late afternoon I was in a hospital room and different people were hovering over me, and all of a sudden my fever spiked to over 103 and I was shaking uncontrollably. A young female doctor tried to take blood from a vein, but she couldn't find one and she stuck me in my arm, my groin and even my foot before giving up. As nice as she was, she was bad at finding veins and it was incredibly painful. She kept apologizing and I kept saying, "That's OK," and taking very deep breaths. Tony watched the whole scene in absolute horror, and when he couldn't take it anymore he nicely asked if she could get someone else to do it. I kept asking for more blankets and continued to tremble uncontrollably.

I was then hooked up to some drugs, and Tony went to

make a few phone calls. A woman entered my room and
started making conversation with me. Something about her
manner made me think she was a social worker, and it was
only after a few minutes I figured out she was a doctor. Dr.
Murray, an infectious disease specialist. When she asked me
to take a deep breath, I could barely breathe without coughing
continuously. "I'm sorry," I said.

"It's OK," she answered.

I felt incredibly guilty about all this and was sure I was to
blame. In her relaxed but extremely precise and professional
manner she listened to my explanation of both my illness and
the cough. I cried that I had told my doctor about it, but
nobody could find anything wrong with me. Dr. Murray answered it was not surprising. The bacteria had hidden in my
system until now, and it wasn't odd that nothing had come up
on any tests. Dr. Murray said she was going to go over my
blood work, try to clearly identify the bacteria and start me on
a course of intravenous antibiotics. I asked her how long I'd
have to stay, but she made it clear I was very sick and we'd
talk about it in a few days. Just as she was leaving, Tony came
in and she gave him a detailed report on her thoughts and also
answered all his questions and then asked him some, not only
about my illness. She was well aware we were far from home
and in need of reassurance, and made it clear she wanted to
take care of both of us. I was so grateful because I knew how
alone Tony felt. She also took my father's phone number and
said she would call him when she finished her rounds.

Later that evening my fever subsided to a little over 101.
Tony stayed late into the night until I finally sent him home.
Then I lay in bed for the rest of the night and completely
freaked out. Around two in the morning a transport person
came to take me for a chest X ray. I'd been meaning to ask

about it, since Dr. Murray had ordered it around six that night, but had finally figured they were going to do it the next morning. I suspect the order had somehow got lost in the shuffle.

It had been only three months since the Northridge earthquake, and the hospital had sustained some damage. I was taken to some sub-basement and left in the X ray room; a nice technician took the picture, and then I was left to wait in the hall for someone to take me back to my room. It was a surreal experience at two in the morning, and I'd say it was the most alone I'd ever felt.

For the rest of the night, except for a few moments of fitful sleep, I stared into the dark. Because of the IV I had to sleep on my back, and I've always slept on my stomach. I waited until exactly 6 A.M. to call Tony and whispered, "When are you coming back?" He said he was just going to order some coffee. I broke down and pleaded with him, "I love you so much and I'm so scared. Please don't let me die." He got the coffee at the hospital. When he arrived, after conferring with the doctors and trying to keep me calm, Tony said, "I called my parents." There was a little crack in his voice that gave away the strain he was under and the fear he tried to keep hidden from me.

By this time the cavalry was coming to the rescue. My father was on a westbound flight, and two of my closest friends, Minna and Debby, both of whom live in L.A., which is the only reason why you haven't heard more about them, were already on their way. One of the first calls to my hospital room came from David Milch. "I just want you to know you've got the job," he said. "You don't have to worry about that." Which of course I had. I figured they were thinking, Oh great, we got ourselves a dying writer on our hands.

Dr. Shaum came to my room early that morning and said the chest X ray showed two emboli (that's plural for embolism, a word in which it is hard to find comfort). "Pneumonia," Doctor Shaum said, but also informed me that was not my real problem. My real problem was the very nasty bacteria that could be treated only with massive doses of intravenous antibiotics. Dr. Murray was trying to find one that worked. The drug I was getting now had been her best guess, but for me to recover she needed to get even more specific. With no fanfare and no desire to scare me, Dr. Shaum said the bacteria had come very close to killing me. It was something I didn't need to be told.

After she left, the thing that most stuck in my mind was that my nurse back in New York had thought she'd seen a shadowy spot on the X ray the week before, and it happened to be where one of the emboli was now lodged. Of course, I blamed myself for not having pursued this. I had a feeling the doctor hadn't scrutinized the X ray.

When my illness had first started three years before, I had run from it. But I'd learned that was not the smartest approach. Now for four months I'd been saying I didn't feel well. But what I hadn't done was trust myself more. I knew my body better than anyone. And I knew what it felt like when it was just plain weak. And though the brutal winter in New York definitely contributed to my not feeling well, I knew it was something more. But I didn't speak up as much as I should have. I had accepted answers that were clinically correct but I felt were wrong. There is nobody to blame for what happened to me. My doctor in New York is one of the premier blood specialists in the world. He explained what was wrong with me, and I accepted the answers because they all fit. Still, I didn't trust those answers, and because I didn't speak up I almost died. I know people throw that expression around loosely, "The doctor said I nearly died," but I didn't need a doctor to tell me, although several did.

Two days later, I was tired and worn-out and the cough was still bad, but my two new doctors said I could go home. That afternoon a home-care nurse would come to the hotel and teach me how to administer the intravenous antibiotics that I would have to take for ten more days. I dreamed of being with Tony in my hotel bed and getting some sleep.

An interesting aside regarding the home care. The company called me at the hospital to check on my insurance and then quoted me a figure for their services. Coincidentally, the case manager from my insurance company called Tony to see how things were going, and he filled her in. She then called the home-care company and got a reduction of one third in the price of the drugs and for the nursing services. "They throw out the highest figure and see if it flies," she later told me. Now, how would anybody think of that. I didn't realize you were supposed to haggle.

Tony had started work the day before, and I told him to keep very quiet about what was going on with me. I didn't want to be perceived as affecting his work. Fortunately, the shooting crew was still in New York and wouldn't arrive for a few weeks, by which time this would all be over and nobody had to know about it.

My father had now arrived, and he and my friend Minna took me home from the hospital. I was completely exhausted and shaking a little bit. When the home-care nurse came to administer antibiotics, she took my temperature, which was back to 101 after two days of no fever. She had to call Dr. Murray, but not to worry, she said, it wasn't that high. Dr. Murray disagreed. She said to have any fever with the amount of antibiotics she was pouring into me was a bad sign, and I had to go right back to the hospital. I begged and pleaded and said I would do anything not to go back, but at most three hours after I'd left I was back in a bed at UCLA. When I called Tony at work to tell him the bad news, I started crying, "But what about my car? We're paying for it and I can't even drive it. Maybe you should return it."

"Don't worry," he answered. "We'll keep it for when you get out."

Clearly, I was a little out of my mind.

Back at the hospital, Dr. Murray had arranged for a room the size of a football field, with carpeting, a couch and chairs, and a nice view of the hills above Bel Air. I swear I never even asked for a private room, and here I had the Joan Crawford suite. Dr. Murray and Dr. Shaum explained the bacteria was more aggressive than they'd originally thought and they needed to observe me while they tried a course of treatment that involved two different antibiotics. Both doctors agreed my port would have to be removed, which was pretty much the ultimate blow. They explained my port was a foreign object, and they were pretty sure the bacteria had already set up shop there. My port had made it possible for me to get all those transfusions, and now they wanted to take it away. It was as much a victim of the bacteria as I was.

The surgeon who was going to perform the procedure, a big bear who had played center on Stanford's basketball team, gave me the reassurance I needed. He also told me I wouldn't be getting a new one until after my body showed no sign of infection. "After we take out the port, I'll put a tempo- rary central line in your neck." A line is a thin tube connected to a vein. My temporary line would go in at the base of my neck and then off it would be three clear thin tubes, like tributaries of a river, through which different medications can be administered.

The next morning the surgeon removed my port and inserted the temporary line. The whole time, he took considerable care in letting me know what he was doing and that everything was fine.

I had hardly been running a fever for days, maybe because they were emptying a few hundred gallons of antibiotics into my system. Tony came to the hospital each night after work and stayed until he was falling asleep. The hospital offered to put a bed in my room, and Tony said he would stay if I wanted him to, and I wanted him to desperately, but felt it wasn't fair. He was handling the pressure incredibly well, and I thought the least I could do was let him sleep at the hotel.

After he left each night I would give him enough time to get home and then would call and cry. In the morning I knew exactly what time he got up, so I'd call and cry. After I hung up one morning at six, my father, an even earlier riser, called and asked, "Why are you doing this to poor Tony?"

"Because I have to," I answered.

My father knew enough to leave it alone.

On a quiet Sunday afternoon, my father and Tony had just left the hospital, and I was in my tenth-floor room with a glorious view of mansions and mountains in the near distance, hanging with my friend Josephine. All of a sudden my bed began to shake and jump off the ground. I figured I'd accidentally hit the controls and something had gone bonkers. As I was trying to figure out the controls I blurted, "What's going on?"

"An earthquake," she answered as the building, which is constructed on rollers, began to sway back and forth violently. It was an aftershock of the Northridge quake and registered

5.6 on the Richter scale. Man, this L.A. trip was turning out to be one disastrous vacation.

A few minutes later my friend Minna arrived, shaken. She had been in the lobby when the quake struck. "All I could do was curse uncontrollably," said Minna. "It was like I had Tourette's syndrome. When it was over I look around and there are these two little kids staring up at me."

My father and Tony had been in the underground parking lot at the time the earth moved, and they watched all the cars jump and all the car alarms go off at the same time. Tony later reported that my father had considered it a particularly unpleasant experience.

That Wednesday was the day before my birthday. I had been running no fever for many days and felt weak, but much better. I was coughing much less, and X rays showed my lungs were clearing up. I begged Dr. Murray and Dr. Shaum to let me go home. They were close to relenting, but were reluctant. Finally I said, "I will say anything to get out of here. I'll shamelessly bribe you and play on any emotion. I'll even lie. So it's probably better if you don't listen to me and do what you feel is best."

Dr. Murray said she felt terrible about keeping me in, but said, "I couldn't live with myself if I let you out and you had to come back. I just couldn't take it." What was I going to say to that?

The Heart of the Matter

On my birthday, I awoke bright and early, made my crying phone call to Tony and got ready to face one of my last days in the hospital. On their early morning visit, my two doctors told me they wanted me to have an echocardiogram just as a precaution. The bacteria in my system, which had been identified as *Hemophilus para-aphrophilus*, like to attack the valves. But both doctors added, "All indications are your heart is fine."

So I was wheeled down to another basement room, where they put some kind of cold jelly and suction cups on my chest and hooked me up to a machine that showed lots of colors on a screen and made a whooshing sound, which was the blood flowing through the heart. Isn't this nifty, I thought.

I chatted up the technician during the test, trying to extract information about what was going on. Toward the end she got a little quiet and I got a lot uneasy. I sneaked a look at my report and saw that the technician had written there was some leakage of the third tricuspid valve. I kept repeating the phrase in my head so I could remember it. My father was waiting outside the door, and when I came out I did what I'd become very good at. I sobbed. At this point I would have made a great extra in funeral scenes on soap operas.

"The worst-case scenario is open heart surgery and you wouldn't want that," the handsome young cardiologist who grew up in Stuyvesant Town told me a short while later as I sat on the side of my bed. "And it's happened in the best place," he continued. "You can live fine without that particular valve." Here we go. They're after my body parts again. And this time it's my heart. "There's a little vegetation on the heart valve," he went on. "But it's not bad. If it were bad it would look like cauliflower. This is just a little thickness on the side of the valve, and we're sure the antibiotics will take care of it. It'll probably disappear completely." Endocarditis is what he called this infection. I call it the scariest thing that had ever happened to me. And I'd been through some scary stuff by this time. Until this point, my heart was something I'd counted on to be fine. I now know when you're sick, you can count on nothing.

And poor Tony. He was working unbelievably hard trying to complete the sets before Nora and the shooting crew arrived in L.A., and I think this final blow finished him off. He kept telling me everything was fine, that he'd spoken to all the doctors and they assured him I was going to be OK. Fortunately, my father, Tony's biggest fan, was looking out for him. The doctors said I could go home the next day, but I was going to have to stay on the intravenous antibiotics for the next five weeks. The home-care nurses would come several times a week and change the bandages where the central line went in at the base of my neck.

So I spent my thirty-seventh birthday in the hospital with

my family and friends. My stepmother, who had arrived a few days before, brought me boxes of beautiful gifts. Tony didn't get me anything, but for once it was hardly important. He was my gift.

But he didn't arrive empty-handed. He brought a gift from someone else. Giorgio Armani.

Mr. Armani has a clipping service that sends him articles that mention his name. He received my article about wanting the suit but giving it up in favor of blood donations. Mr. Armani doesn't speak or read English, but his niece translated my story for him. He was so moved by it he said he would like to make me, someone he had never met, a birthday gift of a suit.

So now Tony stood before me with a cream-colored garment bag emblazoned with Armani's full name on the front. It was accompanied by a simple Happy Birthday note. Before I even unzipped the bag, my stepmother offered, "I'll get you the shirt." I was raking it in. But inside the bag, not only was there an exquisite tightly patterned black and white silk-and-wool pantsuit on black velvet hangers, which also bore Giorgio's name, but also a simple black silk shirt with a detailed pleat on the pocket. "What are you going to say in your thank-you note?" Tony asked.

"I'm gonna say, 'Yo, Giorgio, I gots a birthday every year.' "

The next day I was allowed to go home, driven by Tony in my Mustang convertible. During this time he had stayed on schedule at work, and except for his right-hand man, John Grimolizzi, and our friend Bill Groom, the film's production designer, nobody knew anything about what was going on. But even those two really had no idea. By now the shooting crew had arrived, but I was back at the hotel, and there was no need for anyone to know about what Tony and I had just been through.

A few hours after I came back to the hotel, the home-care nurse arrived. I had to keep to the strict antibiotic schedule. I was taught to administer two different antibiotics, gentamicin and ampicillin, through the two thin tubes coming out of my neck. I ran the connecting tube under my shirt, and the gentamicin was hooked up to a small computerized pump the size of a Walkman, which I wore in a fanny pack around my waist. I have always detested those nylon packs people wear around their waists. You can only imagine what I think of them now. For the other drug, three times a day for forty-five minutes a session, I would hook myself up to an IV pole and run the gentamicin. I was a living science experiment.

That was the hard part, now comes the tricky part. We had emptied the minibar and stocked it with the bags of drugs. But the drugs could only be stored for two days at a time. Three times a week more drugs would be delivered to me at the hotel.

Now, here I am at this very luxurious hotel by the sea. I don't know what they thought when Toni, the delivery person from the home-care services company, came barreling through the lobby with a pole, a red plastic container with the words BIOHAZARD emblazoned on it in bright orange, and thin plastic bags stuffed with syringes and drugs all sticking out the top. For one second I thought of giving Toni fancy shopping bags and asking her to put the drugs in them. I'm middle-class. Appearances are everything. But one look at Toni and the thought of asking her to carry a Barney's bag no longer seemed like the greatest idea. She was a large woman, probably five nine and weighing in at a good 180, mostly muscle, who walked with a swagger that was perfect for what she hoped would be her next profession—on one of her deliveries, Toni informed me that she felt her future is in law enforcement. Did I mention she packed a gun because a lot of the deliveries she made were in tough neighborhoods? Three times a week Toni delivered my supplies to the hotel and walked through the sedate wood-paneled lobby filled with quite the A-list crowd.

By the middle of the second week I called Tony at work and asked if that evening he would stop at the front desk and casually mention that I was receiving deliveries of antibiotics. I was sure that if I were one of the people at the front desk, I'd be thinking this chick has AIDS, and I didn't want them to think that. In fact more than half of the home-care patients in Los Angeles do suffer from AIDS.

It didn't matter because as I was working in the room that very afternoon a call came from the front desk. There was a letter for me, and they were sending it up. It was from my aunt in New York, and she had used an envelope from work. In the upper left-hand corner, printed in bold black ink were the words "N.Y. State Office of Alcohol and Substance Abuse Services."

"Do me a favor," I said to Tony. "Don't stop at the desk on your way home." That night I felt a little relief. "Well, I guess they just think I'm a drug addict."

"Oh, no," Tony replied. "They think you're a drug addict with AIDS."

Have I mentioned the glorious deck overlooking the ocean or the roaring blaze in the lobby fireplaces in the evening? I would have enjoyed them more if I hadn't felt compelled to skulk by the front desk like a criminal. Don't get me wrong. The entire staff was extremely nice, even if I did get a few sideways glances when I said my name.

I usually tried to be in the room when Toni made her delivery, but once I had a doctor's appointment at the same time. When I returned to the hotel, I walked up to the front desk and said quietly to a young woman, "I was expecting a delivery this afternoon."

"Yes, Ms. Breslin," she answered. "It's down in the kitchen. The sticker on the bags said they needed to be refrigerated. Would you like me to have someone send them up?"

"Uh, yes, thank you," I answered meekly.

A few minutes later a room service waiter arrived at my door with two thin plastic bags stuffed with two bags of drugs and my name written in Magic Marker in larger letters across and big orange MUST REFRIGERATE stickers.

I won't go into detail about what it was like to be in a quiet elevator with David Letterman when the pump kicked in and made a whirring sound that caused everyone to look at me, or when the low battery alarm went off as I stood next to Steven Spielberg and his family while waiting for a table at one of the hotel's restaurants.

At least with the parking attendants my reputation was salvaged. My car was listed under my married name, Dunne, so they always called me Mrs. Dunne. To them I had no connection to Ms. Breslin, for whom a gun-toting delivery woman dropped off bags of drugs. And I did find a use for the fancy shopping bags. I'd put all the nonhazardous debris connected to my illness in knotted plastic bags and then placed them in pretty shopping bags next to the garbage can. Whatever else anyone may have thought about me, at least they knew I had good taste. The maids who cleaned our room were so nice to me, and this was way before Tony started peeling off money as thanks.

And in a very short time, I looked like the healthiest person

imaginable. I kept my shirts buttoned so you couldn't see my
central line. Otherwise, I'd gotten a little bit of a tan, was
relatively thin and still had some good muscle tone. No one
would have guessed that I'd almost died a few weeks before.
It's been both a blessing and a curse that I always manage to
look better than I feel. It makes me stronger, but often denies
me some of the sympathy I feel I deserve.

By the way, just a few days after I was happily ensconced
back at the hotel and was clearly recovering, my father and
Ronnie blew out of there as quickly as possible. My father
makes Woody Allen look as if he loves L.A.

The oddest part is, despite all that had gone on, I was
having a great time. In the evenings I would pick Tony up at
work and we'd go for long drives in my convertible. Most
evenings we'd just cruise the Pacific Coast Highway, but
sometimes we'd explore canyons or just pick random roads
and check out the houses. We spent some time with my
friends, some time with people on the movie, but mostly we
spent our time together.

One night, while driving, my lap got incredibly hot. I
opened the fanny pack and saw that my spare set of batteries
was on fire. Tony had always said that I could just look at an
electronic object and cause it to malfunction, and now, as I
was slapping my lap, he exclaimed, "The final proof. The
final proof."

On these nights, we would drive for several hours, and I'd
ask him all about his day and I'd babble about nothing. We
were both trying to rejuvenate in the calm after the storm.
Only I could really detect the signs of strain in Tony. He had
shown that he'd be as strong as the situation required, something I'd always known he would be. But when I was at my
sickest, I'd seen the heartbreak in his eyes and I'd known how

helpless he felt even though he could never know how the nights he'd lain beside me in my hospital bed before he returned to the hotel had saved my soul and my sanity. I had clung to him then, but now, no longer so desperate, I'd let go a little, and Tony and I were joined in a pleasant embrace. We had come through changed but unscathed. How deeply Tony slept at night was a real indication of the pressure he'd been under.

During the days, aside from trips to my various doctors and getting my biweekly blood transfusions—remember, I still had my good old blood disorder—I started work with David Milch on my *N.Y.P.D. Blue* script, read books by the pool, and rode a rented bike a few miles down the beach path to Venice, where the film was shooting, to stop and give Tony a kiss. My friends came to visit me at the hotel. After our evening drives, Tony and I either went out to eat or returned to our room and ordered room service. We had quite a little bill going. During all this time the most intimate act we performed was our daily ritual of Tony taping me up with plastic so when I showered water didn't get under the bandage where the central line entered my neck. You can imagine how sexy and vibrant I felt with these things hanging out of me, but still one night I broached the topic of sex.

"I didn't think you were interested."

"Well, I am," I said.

"All right."

Two days passed and still I waited. Finally, I broke down and sobbed. "You haven't said anything. It's not that I'm really interested in sex. I just want to feel normal, do something normal. I can't understand all that I've been through and I just thought that there's one thing I can do only with you and I need to know I'm not just this sick person."

"I was just waiting to be a little spontaneous," Tony answered.

"Spontaneous," I said in utter shock. "I've got these tubes hanging from my neck, I'm hooked up to a minicomputer that automatically pumps antibiotics into my system for one hour out of every four so I'd have to disconnect it for a period of time. I also have to time when I take the other drug, so I don't think spontaneity is an issue here."

"I guess not," he answered lamely. Just in case you were starting to think he's too perfect.

I loosened things up with a couple of sick jokes about some kinky things we could do with the tubes. Tony had to admit we actually had a little fun. I did get a little sentimental and cry in the middle, but that was good.

A few weeks before we left L.A. I finished with the antibiotics, my heart valve had returned to normal and the central line was removed, and a new port was surgically implanted. That was not a lot of fun and I spent a few days in bed, but after all I'd been through I wouldn't let it get to me. I spent the better part of the last few days hanging in the swimming pool because I was finally allowed in the water.

I was reluctant to leave my happy home. Later, back in New York, when somebody who didn't know what had happened, asked, "How was L.A.?" I spontaneously answered, "It was great. We had the best time."

End of Part III

Let's Wrap This Baby Up

After we returned to New York, it seemed the worst was over. I was still sucking up blood, and every so often as I walked around I'd think, The only reason I'm alive is because of strangers' blood in my body. I used to look at the bags—it says where they're from—and they would be from Oklahoma City, St. Louis and Tampa. Rarely is blood from New York because people here don't donate blood. It's a problem in most large cities. I think people should get a few bucks off their taxes for each pint donated. It's a safe guess that would put a dent in the problem. In the meantime New York hospitals purchase their blood from other parts of the country. You get a lot from army bases. Soldiers may even be required to donate.

While I was contemplating blood, Tony had immediately started work on *Die Hard: With a Vengeance*. He caught an afternoon flight from L.A. and started the next morning in New York, working six and seven days a week constructing huge sets, often until eight or nine at night. They were shooting on weekends, which is much easier in the city in the summer, so he always worked at least part of a Saturday and Sunday and at best had a Tuesday off. We'd rented a beach house to which he never came, and Tony kept saying it was ridiculous for me to stay in the city, which was now as brutally hot as it had been cold the winter before. Anemics don't do well in temperature extremes, and the heat was really wearing me out. I was quiet about it, but I was pretty miserable. The best the blood made me feel was sluggish. But my complexion once again was beautiful, with that pale, porcelain look, on which people often commented. Maybe I've stumbled upon a new beauty secret. Go and lose a few pints of blood and you're on your way.

For several years, different doctors had discussed the possibility of using a procedure called plasmapheresis. This procedure involves hooking up the patient to a high-tech machine, sucking out large quantities of blood through one tube, spinning the blood through the machine and taking out the plasma, substituting it with some man-made plasma, which is then mixed with the blood cells and put back into the patient through a second tube.

My port could not be used for this latest treatment because doctors were afraid it would blow out, sort of like a tire. So, to my complete dismay, a catheter was temporarily placed in my chest. This was slightly different from the tubes hanging out of my neck in L.A., but it was still things hanging from my body, which wasn't a lot of fun, although the catheter would be removed after ten days. In a half-hour procedure, a really cute doctor stuck these tubes in my chest and he was feeling sorry for me because all I could do was cry. Still, in between tears I managed to ask, "Are you married?"

"Yes, why?" he asked.

"I was just wondering," I answered. Actually, Abigail was out in the waiting room, and I'd figured I could introduce them. Let no opportunity go unexploited.

The theory behind this plasmapheresis was that perhaps this antibody that was attacking my red blood cells could be filtered out during the procedure. This wouldn't be a cure, but the antibody would be reduced enough that my body would function normally for a time and then I could do the plasmapheresis again many months down the line. It seemed worth a shot to me. The vampire bit was wearing thin.

So the cute doctor stuck a tube in my chest early on a Monday morning in late June, and about an hour later I was shipped downstairs and hooked up to the machine for five hours, which was done each day for one week. Once I was hooked up to this machine with all kinds of tubes and bottles, I was a little freaked out. As they stood around me in the room, even Tony, my father and Ronnie had a hard time pretending this was not extremely disconcerting. "My life as a science experiment," I joked to the crowd.

"You must have a good diet," a nurse said as a big plastic bag filled with my plasma.

"Huh?" I answered.

"Well, yours is very clear. If you had a bad diet it would be cloudy, sort of milky." I always love how healthy everyone tells me I am. Once the doctor had returned with test results and said I had the best cholesterol levels of anyone in the office. "That's great," my father shot back. "Except she's got no red blood."

But here we were again, everyone telling me how healthy I was as I sat attached to a machine out of a sci-fi flick. On the first day I made the mistake of drinking a lot of coffee while I was hooked up, and discovered I couldn't get up and go to the bathroom. In an emergency a nurse will bring a bedpan. "No way," I said, and for the last hour it was so bad that I told Tony he couldn't talk to me. At least the acute discomfort took my mind off how weird this was and I took a little break from crying. When I talk about all the crying I've done, most of it had been done in private. Everyone I've dealt with has always been impressed with my strength, but now I had nothing left. It had been more than a year since I'd felt well and it had finally caught up to me, and this new stuff was really exhausting.

I used to save the tears for home and Tony, but now I was so tired and worn-out and the catheter left my chest feeling so sore that I was feeling very sorry for myself and intended to cry quite a bit. I'd had no time to recover from my ordeal in L.A. This was all happening less than a month after I was taken off the intravenous antibiotics, and here I was immediately on to something else.

Also, I am the Queen of the Delayed Reaction. Tony says I can get through anything, no matter how difficult, and it only registers much later. I imagine this is quite common. So here I was reacting to the months before, while something new was already on the line. I had quite a backlog of depression, and I was ready to cash in.

I believe in setting a scene, which I certainly was doing. And as I now felt the importance of doing all things as best you can, I intended to excel at depression. I went to see a shrink and made her cry, so I'd say I was off to a good start.

For the five days I had plasmapharesis and for the five days more that I had to keep the catheter in my chest—the cute doctor thought it needed to heal a little before he pulled it out or else I might bleed excessively—I spent every afternoon and evening as well as the weekend in bed. I had one T-shirt and sweats that I wore pretty much the entire time. I spent a few hours each day on my *N.Y.P.D. Blue* script, and then watched soap operas on TV and ate reheated Chinese food as summer scenes played out outside my window.

One afternoon a little rice stuck to the comforter cover, but I thought it really rounded out the picture, so I left it there. By the third afternoon I had spilled a little brown sauce on the front of my V-neck Hanes T-shirt, from which I had hung the two tubes. It was more comfortable that way, kind of like when guys unbutton the top of their jeans. It was also a little slovenly, which drove home my point when Tony returned. When you look like that, you don't need words to get across how you're feeling. All the time I hear people say proudly of someone who is quite ill, "She never complains. She never says, 'Why me?' " I say these people never heard the complaints or else the sick person is a moron. Because when something truly horrible happens to you, you've got to be out of your mind not to say, "Why me?" Sure, I am discreet about who hears these words or sees my tears, but they are there. When something fantastic happens to someone and they're not overjoyed, we think their behavior is strange. Yet, if something horrible happens, you're a hero if you act as if nothing's wrong. I say screw that. I'm not happy, and I'm going to let you know it. Of course, as all of us sick people know, when the true test comes, when you've got to have surgery or chemotherapy or blood transfusions, when you've got to be poked, pricked, prodded or plasmapharesed, you use every ounce of strength in your body to get through it and survive. But in the off season, I think depression, self-pity and taking to one's bed are highly underrated and have an unjustifiably bad rap.

I'm not recommending depression as a way of life—I'm a

true believer in the mind/body connection—but just as an occasional time-out. I could no longer hide my depression from my friends and family, as if it were something to be ashamed of. I was out of the closet. I tried to tell my friends and family how I felt, but in between the sobs most of the words were incomprehensible. Of course, Maria and Abigail and our other close friends Kristin and Suzanne took this time to tell me I don't talk to them enough about my feelings. So while I was now sharing my fears, I was getting in trouble for holding them back in the past. Because I am in so many ways a showman, I forget how much I keep within. "You never talk about how you feel," Maria said with mock annoyance. But my perception was that I had unburdened myself on all my friends.

It was during this time, when I was feeling good and sorry for myself, that my nurse Ann Culkin, who specializes in the large tumor group, introduced me to Isabelle. "You've got to talk to her," Ann said. "She feels so alone and that everyone else is so old and I know it'll help."

"Don't do this to me. I told you no more terminals," I answered, already walking into Isabelle's room. Her face was blown up from the steroids, but beneath you could see she was a great Italian beauty. We got to talking easily. She was not even thirty, had never smoked a cigarette and now had inoperable lung cancer. All I did was tell her of my feelings and desires and what I felt about what I'd been living through. That summer she went to Lourdes and brought me back a card she'd had blessed while she prayed for me. She married that fall and fought on, and exactly two years after we first met she died from the cancer that had spread to her bones and brain.

I keep promising myself I'm going to walk into this building and not look to my left or right, just straight ahead and not make eye contact with anyone. It's too hard. But I can't. And as much as meeting someone like Isabelle tears at my insides, I can't pretend she's not there. Somehow we helped each other, even if just a little.

A few days after I was finished with the plasmapharesis the cute doctor pulled the catheter out of my chest. I mean, literally pulled, as in one-two-three yank and a flash of blinding pain. But then it was all over. Of course, within several days it was also apparent the plasmapharesis hadn't worked. Or at least, not the way the doctors had hoped it would.

In a total shot in the dark, crapshoot, my doctor thought enough of the antibody attacking my red blood cells had been filtered out and I might once again be responsive to the gamma globulin, so I resumed my treatment schedule. And it worked great. My blood count soared into the normal range, which meant no more biweekly blood transfusions. I was back to three five-hour days at the hospital every month, which was fine with me.

But the biggest thing was I felt well. It absolutely transformed my whole life. Finally, after a horrible fifteen months something was going right. But I was too worn-out to show my appreciation, too scared to trust it and still pretty shell-shocked.

At least I now had my work. I was fairly well along on a script for *N.Y.P.D. Blue.* But one summer afternoon a week after I finished the plasmapharesis, I got a call from David Milch, who told me to stop writing. David Caruso was leaving the show after the fourth episode of the second season, to be replaced by Jimmy Smits. My script had to be rewritten because the new character was going to be quite different from Caruso's.

I threw away what I'd written, and after Milch told me some of his ideas for the new character, I started to rethink the script. The only problem was there would be roughly a six-week delay before I could start again because he had to create the new character and write the three scripts that would familiarize the audience with him. I still had my *Newsday* columns to write, but otherwise my schedule for the bulk of the summer was now completely empty. And I was lost without Tony. He was working all the time building big sets that would be blown up, and as the months dragged on, the only thing he could do on his occasional day off was sleep. I was really healthy for the first time in so long, but I wouldn't let myself trust it. There's a picture of me from that summer, paddling out in Gardiner's Bay in a sea kayak, tanned and strong and looking like an Olympic athlete. All right, maybe a high school gym teacher. But though my body felt Olympian that summer, I worried it was temporary and I was a little bit afraid of it. I almost didn't know what to do with it. And here I was finally at the fun part, and I couldn't share it with the one person I wanted to.

Fortunately, at the end of the summer my work schedule picked up fast. After all the delays, my script had to be written quickly. As for Tony, after he finished *Die Hard* he took three days off, during which he slept and fielded phone calls before he began work on another movie with monstrous sets called *Money Train.*

On a frigid fall Saturday I drove out to the MTA's Coney Island Overhaul Yard transit authority repair yard, where Tony's crew was building the subway trains that picked up the money from the token booths. Tony had taken old trains and completely reconditioned them into shining steel bullet-proof cars with floodlights and gun ports in the sides. I had been riding the New York subways on my own since I was a kid and Peggy Doran and I would sneak off on the GG local to the Alexander's department store on Sixty-third Drive. I believe I've been on every line at every hour of the day or night.

"How is it I've never even seen anything like these cars?" I asked Tony of this moving metal army base.

"That's because it doesn't exist. You know the yellow garbage trains?" he asked, referring to the run-down, derelict-looking subway cars that chug through the stations. "Well, that's what the real money train looks like, but nobody's going to want to watch a whole movie with that as a centerpiece. It would make for a really exciting and visual chase scene, don't you think?" he added, smiling slyly.

I left Tony to building his fantasy subway cars, and I remained the slightly pathetic creature I am when he works that hard, even though I now had to make several trips to L.A. to work on my script. At one point I had to stay in L.A. for ten days. I was doing so much silent fretting that Tony finally asked, "What is going on?" I confessed the only way I could successfully accomplish the trip was if he came out for the weekend. I had calculated that, at the most, the number of nights I would be alone in L.A. would be four, which I could handle. More than that was questionable. "I'll never make it more than that without you." I knew the last thing Tony wanted to do after an eighty-hour workweek was jump on a plane, but he liked my flirtation with work and employment, so he bought a plane ticket.

I was finally moving toward finishing the script—my episode number, not surprisingly, was thirteen—when smack in the middle of a morning meeting with David Milch I got a call from my brother Patrick in New York.

My father had an aneurysm in his brain. Of course, he

doesn't get some wimpy thing like what I get. He goes for the gold. I'd always known he was going to steal the attention away from me in this whole illness thing. He was trying to do that with his "Let me exchange my life for yours" performance in the wings all those years. More doctors, nurses, other patients, family and friends have all said, "This must be so hard on your father." But now he had moved front and center stage. The aneurysm was found by accident and it did not erupt. Successful brain surgery was performed, and after one of the briefest states of grace we all agreed he came back meaner than ever. As for his brain, it was as sharp as it had always been. This was greeted with great relief, but not great surprise. Of course, my father and I had joked about what we would do if he came out a drooling lug.

"You're Ronnie's problem" was my contribution.

As the months passed and my health remained relatively good I started to trust it enough to have a complete emotional breakdown. An issue that had started before Tony and I got married rose right back to the surface. Birthing babies.

When we first got married I tried to get pregnant, outfitted with both an ovulation kit and an early pregnancy test. We tried unsuccessfully for six months, at which point my health deteriorated and getting pregnant got lost in the struggle to stay alive.

"Maybe we should just drive to West Virginia and try to buy a baby or hire a stranger to carry the baby for us. Pay somebody," I said one day.

After our initial attempts were not successful and my health became a major concern, whenever I talked about getting pregnant Tony brought up the practical part, such as what if I became sick and couldn't take care of a baby or if something happened to me, who would help him with a child and could he afford it and what if he's got a crazy work schedule or a location job. These are all real issues, but I didn't want to acknowledge them, and I'd either get nasty or make him feel like a brute for bringing them up. Basically, that was just another one of my tactics. "Well, what would I do with a baby if something happened to you?" Tony asked, finally.

"Lots of people do it," I answered. "And wouldn't it be better to have a part of me than nothing. Anyway, you keep saying I'm going to be fine and I'm not going to die, so what's the problem?"

"That's what I have to say," Tony answered quietly.

I also resented that unless I brought up the topic he let it lie dormant at his feet. I knew how afraid he was, but at that point I only cared about how I felt. And this was tearing at my core. The first time the wave of emotional pain hit me I had no idea what it was about. Was it my mother? Being sick? I didn't know what was tearing apart my insides and leaving such a deep pain in a very particular spot front and center at the top of my rib cage. I could really feel it. With this pain came every mix of emotions. On the subject, my head and heart often wandered in wild directions. At one point I wanted a baby so badly I blurted to Tony, "I don't care if I die having a baby," which upset him more than a little.

"I don't care," I cried in the front seat of the car on the L.I.E. "You'll probably end up without me anyway. This way you'll have something." And I meant it. I worry constantly about Tony without me and I can't help feeling that a baby, part of us, would make it easier for him. "This sounds like something that happens in a soap opera," I added, sniveling. "And not even one that's doing good in the ratings." Helpful friends and family have all said, "You can always adopt." And they mean well. And maybe I will. I know I would never love one child more than another, but what I'm saying is I'm still at the point where I want my own. Not that I would consider an adopted child less than my own, but it's a subtle difference only another woman in my position could truly understand. Wanting a child and wanting your own child are two distinct things, and I think that only after I've resolved my feelings about the first can I seriously consider the second.

After we returned from Los Angeles, before we tried the plasmapharesis, my doctor discussed the possibility of another chemotherapy treatment. "If we do it, don't try getting pregnant," he advised. Later, when I couldn't stop crying my father said, "Go shopping. Spend a lot of money on clothes." My stepmother looked at him. "She doesn't want to go shopping, Jimmy. She wants a baby." Without skipping a beat, he answered, "Well then, go to West Virginia and buy one." This West Virginia thing must run in the family. And don't tell me it's social conditioning, this is pure genes.

After the plasmapharesis and the start of my new good health another chapter in the baby saga began. Now that I felt well for the first time in so long I wasn't ready to try to get pregnant, which doctors had all said was possible, but could be quite difficult. The thought of being sick, increased treatments and near-daily doctor visits brought such a heaviness on me that the thought of it made me want to crawl in bed and eat a pint of Häagen-Dazs vanilla chocolate almond. I was racked by guilt about this and felt like a horrible person, considering how strongly I had insisted I wanted a baby. I began to think maybe I had never really wanted a baby, that I had just been playing up the melodrama.

But I knew that wasn't true. There were still times, when I'd be walking on the street or on the checkout line at the supermarket when the pain would hit, and I'd know what it was. Sometimes a sadness would settle on me and other times a series of slow sobs. Sometimes I'd be watching TV with Tony, and I'd just start to cry. Once it was in the middle of a Dorito's commercial, and even then Tony knew immediately what it was about. I was almost keening. "I feel like I really failed you," he said. I had never wanted him to feel that way, and I admitted I'd resisted all his concerns because they'd been mine as well, and that this wasn't my decision alone and that we had to support each other. And, after all, there is the real possibility that he may end up a single parent, so shouldn't he have a big say in the decision? And though Tony acted as if he could take on anything, he now had to admit, "I don't know if I can handle more. It takes everything I've got to take care of you, to work, and to keep myself sane, and I'm afraid I couldn't handle any more pressure. I think it would just push me over the edge." I could hear in his voice once again that he felt this was a failing. I let him know that though I wished it were different, it wasn't, and this had nothing to do with failure. This was real life at its hardest, and nobody but us could understand all that was involved. And it was an issue that so easily could have divided us, especially since I was often out of my mind with baby fever. But when I saw how Tony couldn't separate my grief from his own feelings of failure I had to stop. It was too hard any other way, and wasn't all this about how much we loved each other?

Sometimes I feel robbed of so many things by this illness, and at other times I accept this wonderful life I now have, and anything else, including a baby, would be more good fortune. As hard as it is at times for me to see that, I really believe it. And the whole time my love for Tony just grows deeper, and isn't that enough of a miracle for one girl?

But that doesn't mean I don't imagine life with my child, that he or she doesn't sit behind me in the baby seat of the Jeep or grab my hand as I walk down the street or go out with Tony. A mother is something I know I am meant to be, though probably will never be. Or maybe it's just that I'll never have my own child. I don't know. I find myself wavering so much on the whole thing. I just have to pray there's a reason for this or at least something positive in my getting sick. Sometimes I scare myself when I think of my illness as being more of a positive than a negative, but I think that's why I'm still alive.

The positive side of my life these last few years has been so overwhelming, obviously personally but also professionally. Once I went back to writing, I wanted to do it only if I could do the best job possible. I'm too old and too worn-out to do something and be left with that sinking feeling that I sort of slid by. I worked as hard as I could on my *N.Y.P.D. Blue* episode, which aired on Valentine's Day and placed in the No. 10 spot for the week. I did the same with each of the *Newsday* columns and used to wait by the phone for the reaction from my number one fan, John Gregory Dunne, who would call first thing in the morning when a column ran. I had finally reached the point where I got from my work what I got from my personal life, and it felt really good.

Of course, my luck being what it is, I was offered an unbelievable job at New York *Newsday* writing twice a week about anything I wanted, and right after the offer New York *Newsday* promptly shut down. Now, I think I should be allowed to consider this a bad break, but I didn't. I was finally smart enough and had lost enough of the arrogance of youth to see that a newspaper hadn't shut down just because I'd been offered a job there. Although the thought did cross my mind.

But I was going to miss those checks for my column. They may have been small, but they were steady. And I had a secret need for that money, one that was exposed one afternoon when Tony saw some canceled checks on my desk. One check was made out to my friend Minna for five hundred dollars. "Why'd you write Minna that check?" he asked innocently.

"I owed her the money," I answered.

"For what?"

I took a deep breath. I wanted Tony to know that my checks from *Newsday* and from *N.Y.P.D. Blue* had not been squandered. He had never asked me what I did with the money, and I assumed he figured I was blowing it because I had remained very guarded about my bank account. Finally, I told him everything. At my lowest point, I had borrowed money from three people very close to me. Quietly, from the first *Newsday* check on, I had been paying everyone back in monthly payments. In addition, I had paid off any other debts I had. Also, for the first time, neither Tony nor my father paid any of the uncovered portion of my medical expenses. I had paid all that myself. I gave Tony a detailed account of where every penny I earned had gone.

Now comes the worst part. He used it against me. Without my realizing it, Tony figured if I was good with all my scams, and now with the responsible repayment of my debts, he could get this to work for him. He ignited my newfound pride in doing the best job possible. And he employed it to make me a solid citizen, something I had sneered at my whole life. Tony set me up and I fell for it. My own husband did this to me. First, he got me to feel I had to prove to him I was good with money. So I started to look at our expenses and figure where we could cut costs, just as I did when I used to pilfer money from him. Only now the savings went in the bank. Next, to expand my knowledge, I started to read about investing and actually read the D section of *The New York Times*. Then came the lowest. Don't ask me how I sank to this point. I bought books on finances. However, I did draw the line at balancing my checkbook. But as I was now good with money, I had a fair grasp of the approximate amount in my account.

Of all the things Tony could do to me, this was the worst. He even made me buy a wallet. I had never been big on wallets, and during my destitute period it seemed a silly thing to carry if you had nothing to put in it. But now I had credit cards, on which I didn't carry balances, so nobody was calling me up and instructing me to cut them up and send them back in the mail. When I went to the cash machine I no longer had the momentary fear that a slip of paper reading "Insufficient funds" would come out. Now I actually had money. This was not the life for me. But I was doing it and getting better and better at it. Although I did say to Tony, "You know I had it a lot better when I was a deadbeat. I didn't work and I got an allowance. Now I work and all my money goes to bills and savings. My deal was much better before. And don't think I don't know it." After he made me invest some of my money from *N.Y.P.D. Blue,* I turned on him. "You stole my money," I said.

He showed me some piece of paper from some mutual fund. "There's your money."

"I don't want some piece of paper with numbers on it. I want cold hard cash and I don't have it. You stole it. Give it back."

But Tony had the hook. He knew I had found myself in my work and wouldn't stop. He also knew I understood how much he wanted to have something to show for all his hard work, so I wouldn't let him down. I couldn't even turn to my sister to commiserate because she too seemed to have gone semi-legit. What's wrong with this world? Doesn't anyone have any fun anymore? But the absolute worst was that Tony had actually scammed me. Me, a professional.

And now I was running around acting like a reformed drug addict or somebody who'd found religion. I began to examine our spending further and advised Tony on habits he could change and talked about different ways to invest.

Fortunately, one day in Bloomingdale's, a glimpse of the real me emerged. There was a beautiful dress I saw and wanted, but it was expensive and I didn't need it and couldn't afford it because Tony and I were now saving for something. Out of an inside pocket of my wallet I pulled out a little-used credit card and paid for the item. Then I quickly took the escalator up to the ladies' lounge and called my father. "I needed to spend some money," I said. "But I didn't feel like spending my own. So I spent yours." He laughed so hard. I had made his day.

What Tony and I were now saving for was a house. A country retreat. I had considered only the ocean, but one late fall weekend we drove to an inn in Washington, Connecticut, and I looked around at the New England town and the rolling hills and turned to Tony and said, "Get me a pair of Wellingtons. I can play this game."

By this time we had looked at many houses in many areas and had even seriously bid on one, but it fell through. We spent this weekend looking at houses and came back a second time. The agent who had taken us out the first time was away, and her colleague, Bumpy, was taking us—oh my God, what was I getting into—to see a few houses and for a second look at one Tony liked and was seriously considering but I was not sold on. I had been working the numbers and thought the carrying costs combined with the improvements necessary were a little steep. An alien being has taken over my brain. Quick, give me five thousand bucks and a plane ticket to Bali and get me out of here. The real me is off globe-trotting and squandering every penny she has.

When we got into Bumpy's car, she asked what we were looking for. After we told her, she said, "That's funny. I saw a house yesterday that sounds like what you're talking about." We drove up steep hills past Revolutionary War homes and fields with open vistas until we reached a working farm. We turned off the main road onto a dirt-packed road, drove through the farmland and down an eighth-of-a-mile stretch. At the bottom of the hill we made a left, and at the end of a long dirt driveway with a stream running under it was a small Cape Cod house with a small beaten-down barn behind it. Brass tacks pounded into the heavy wooden kitchen door said "1757," but in fact the house was built in 1732. It had wide plank floors, beamed ceilings and a large stone fireplace in the living room. The moment we walked in the door I could tell Tony was in love. I liked the house, but was nervous. This was a serious adult purchase. Still, I knew if he loved it I'd be happy. Right then and there Tony said, "We'll take it."

I knew it was right. The house was in good enough shape to live in, but could be slowly transformed. And that's what Tony had been looking for. He so wanted to put all he knew to use on something permanent, and here it was. He took detailed photographs of the house, and later that day he started to work on drawing plans for renovations and interior floor plans. Before we even closed on the house he had six Windsor chairs made. "If we don't get the house, we can hang the chairs on our apartment walls," I advised.

For Tony, buying the house was a dream, and it was fun to watch, but for me it brought conflicting emotions and issues.

My first feeling was I wanted the house to go away. All I'd been through had loosened my grasp just a little more on living, and I was afraid to make a permanent move because I wondered how permanent I was. How could I sit in the living room with Tony and plan our work on the house for the next five years when I wondered if I'd even live that long. But then, I had lived with this for six years, so I couldn't not plan at all. But the recent road had been so rocky, I wondered, How many times can a body go through this and bounce back? As for the issues, there was a major one. I so wanted to play the part of happy couple first-time homeowners, but couldn't. And I felt cheated. As I prepared the mortgage material, I said to Tony, "I don't want my name on this house."

"What do you mean?"

"I mean I don't want to own anything. No car. No house. Nothing. It's a lot easier to keep a name off in the first place than to take it off later."

"What are you talking about?"

"What I'm talking about is if I run into big-time medical expenses. I want to be ready."

This issue had come to me instinctively. My health insurance has a lifetime cap of $1 million. So does Tony's. There's a real possibility that if I live I'll run through both of that. Then what? The government, hospitals and doctors go after everything you've got. You lose it all. I have no problem paying what is fair and what I can, but am I supposed to watch Tony's life be destroyed because of my illness? I do feel there is something wrong when I, who have worked and paid taxes and am a citizen, have to plan to divorce the person who is my whole life rather than risk his losing all he spent his life working for. And divorce is my most extreme option.

We get bills at home for figures such as $40,297.60, most

of which is now covered by insurance. What if we had to pay this? We couldn't. As it is, the uncovered portion of my medical expenses runs upward of $10,000 most years. You try and pay that. We do. But what if the figure was $100,000?

I'm aware of how privileged my situation is already, how much I can rely on my family and friends for help. Nobody could pay the insane amounts my illness costs. What's Tony supposed to do? Lose everything? And what should my father do? Spend the golden years of an artist's life scrambling for dollars for me, which is what he would do?

I have made it very clear to Tony I would walk away from him and never look back before I would let any of this happen. I would separate myself from everybody. And you just can't get a divorce and go on living together or something like that. Our government actually spends money making sure couples who do this are not really together before you qualify for Medicaid and other social services. Yet, in the chemo room one day I sat next to a Russian immigrant who came here knowing he had lung cancer and thought he could get better treatment. He had no money or insurance, so he applied for and received Medicaid and disability money because he could not work. I didn't have the nerve to ask, but he probably also qualified for food stamps and maybe welfare. He also received free car service to and from the hospital. Most years, I spend over $3,000 on taxis, none of which is tax-deductible.

I remember reading in the *Times* that more than half those attending the U.S. Open Tennis Championships at Flushing Meadow were writing off their tickets as a business expense. It just blew my mind that our system allows you to deduct half the price of a tennis ticket or even a part of dinner for tax reasons, but nothing for health unless it is above a certain amount of your gross income. So basically, if you work and try to earn a decent income, you get penalized.

On the day I sat next to the Russian, an elderly couple from New Jersey came in. There was much wringing of hands, and they spoke in urgent, hushed tones to a nurse. But it wasn't over the husband's chemotherapy treatments. It was over the $300 a week it cost them for a taxi from Jersey when the husband receives treatment, $60 each day for his five-day cycle. "We can't afford it," the wife said apologetically to the nurse, who said she would immediately contact a social worker to try to help the couple.

On another afternoon, a retired schoolteacher who is nearing sixty-five, sat across from me. She informed the gang that when she reaches that age she will go off her private health insurance and onto Medicare. "They don't pay for prescriptions," she said. "And I can't afford to pay." She quizzed the nurse about the necessity of continuing her prescription, which the nurse subtly indicated might be the difference between living and dying. No gray areas here, unless you're talking about the pallor of some people's skin. The retired teacher then started seriously speaking about moving to Canada. She said she knew no one there, but heard Toronto wasn't a bad place. "They have national health insurance there," she said. I paid close attention to her.

That night I repeated to Tony, "I'll walk out the door without a glance back before I let this destroy our lives."

"Don't say that," he answered. But I know it is what I would do because I would rather not be alive than make that my life or my husband's. "When the money's gone, love goes out the door," my father jokes, but what he means is that bills and debts and phone calls from people wanting money kill your heart. In hospitals and doctors' offices I've heard people talk more about money than about health. It would be very easy to point the finger at the Russian guy, which is what I initially did, just as many of us have at illegal aliens abusing emergency rooms and poor people using them in place of doctors' visits. It's wrong to do that. But it's wrong of my country to force me to separate from the person whose love has kept me alive. I have no idea what the answers are, but it is an issue with no room for finger pointing or placing blame. The health care system is in such desperate shape I truly believe the only hope is to stop treating it as a political issue and for everyone in all related fields to be seriously involved. It would be a painfully slow procedure, but could have real results. And it's not going to happen.

The interesting thing about my idea not to own anything or have my name on any of our investments is that when I explained why to our lawyer and accountant, neither of them disagreed with me, and they both said it was a particularly savvy move on my part. "That's if you trust Tony with everything," my accountant said, but he knew us and knew the answer. I laughed, because I do. But should I have to? Is this what I should spend my spare time thinking about? The entire medical system is a minefield, and I'm constantly stepping on a mine or just barely missing.

What finally most won me over about buying the house was a sense that I was settling Tony. If I don't live long, I'll know he's taken care of. The house is beautiful. He's already begun to show his incredible abilities, and he says I haven't seen anything yet. But when I open the side door and enter the kitchen, it's as if I enter a world I dreamed up. It's my own little movie set. The most romantic little house in the world. Everything in it is perfect without being precious. I love it so much, and I love it that every time I turn around Tony is building something or restoring something or talking to a plumber, gardener or barn converter. When he finally took a break from work for a few months last summer before starting on the Ron Howard film *Ransom,* he spent the whole time working on the house and the garden and roaming the fields with his chain saw.

One afternoon, while I was watching a basketball playoff game, Tony kept hassling me about the curtains he was hanging and he was not happy with the way they were draping. Finally, I pulled out my wallet, handed him a credit card and said, "Honey, do me a favor. Let me just watch the game for an hour. Why don't you just go wild and order from a few catalogs." Later, I added, "You better have sex with me tonight or I'm gonna know you're gay." What did you think? I'd progressed a little after all this time.

Most afternoons my favorite thing to do was tag along and ask, "What are you doing?" until he sent me on some errand or had me dig a ditch and move a bush. In the late afternoons we'd get in the car and take long drives on back roads without knowing where they led.

On one of these drives I talked about the future. "I don't want you to be alone. It's not for you," I said. "I put so much into you and you're so great and look what you've got to offer. You're too good to waste." He tried to cut in, but I made it clear I had to say these things.

I feel in this whole world there would never have been anyone for me but Tony Dunne. I know it and anyone who knows me knows it. It's a fact. So he must be a gift from God. I cannot be the awful person I sometimes feel I am if I've been given someone so wonderful. And if someone has so prospered from my love, there must be some real good in me.

I want to be old with him, live my life with him, have him listen to all the silly thoughts that pass through my head. But that may not happen. And my heart begs, Please, someone take care of him. He's such a loner. He won't reach out for somebody. He thinks there's only me even though I tell him there's not. "They'll never be someone like me, but there are a few great women out there, which, by the way, is not something I can say about men, and I want you to be with one of these women," I've told Tony.

What would the house be like alone? What would he do at night? He doesn't like to go out. All he'd do is eat Chinese food. Who would make him oatmeal in the morning? He likes grapefruit juice, Quaker Instant Maple with added raisins, and coffee. I hardly ever miss a day making him breakfast, even when he's got a 5 A.M. call. Who would do this for him? And, in return, whom would he build beautiful things for?

Trust me, the babe who lands this guy doesn't know what she's in for. He's smart and cool and tough, but he'll spend weeks deliberating over fabric swatches, and though I make fun of it, wait and see what you get in the end. If you think I've given such a detailed description of our country home for no reason, guess again. I may no longer be able to scam, but at least let me have an ulterior motive. What I was doing was juicing up the package. You don't have to read Jane Austen to know the importance of a man with property. Landed gentry. That's my guy.

I just don't want him to be alone. Even now, I still feel a little guilty about letting him fall so in love with me when the chances of a long ride are slim. I've made Tony promise he won't try to stay alone, that it would be such a waste for him and all the hard work I've put into him. I made Maria swear she would look out for him. "I don't care if he meets someone the day after I die," I told her. "I don't want him to be unhappy. And if you don't do this for me I'll consider it an act of betrayal." Got her right then and there, which was my intent.

"You're a much better person than I am," she answered. "If anything should happen to me, you better make sure Kenneth is unhappy. And if he even looks at another woman in less than a year . . ." She tried to strong-arm me into the one-year plan for Tony, but I said no, she should start trying from the moment it's certain I'm not going to make it, if that should happen. To Tony, I've given a short list of potential candidates, just a few women I feel are right. He doesn't like to listen to me, but I know he likes all my choices, except for one of my top ones, his cousin Quintana, who is not related by blood. He loves her, but she is fourteen years younger and he used to babysit for her. "I remember when Quintana was a little girl," he said.

"Well, she's not anymore," I answered. "She's all woman."

"You're picking the people you want," Tony replied.

"Who am I gonna pick? Anyway," I added. "I don't really have to. They'll be coming after you."

I figure that as much as a loner Tony is, women will be after him before he even knows it. I told him to consider someone in the movie business so she would understand the hours.

I pray none of this happens, but in these seven years so many things have happened. But I'm still standing. Still nobody knows what's wrong with me or if it's going to become something worse and this is just the precursor for the real thing. Recently, when some other numbers involving blood counts were below normal, my doctor said nonchalantly, "I always thought this may someday show itself to be red blood cell cancer." It might have been nice if somebody had mentioned it to me, but hey, man, I'd be a moron if a thought like that hadn't passed through my little head. And there continue to be rocky periods, though the last two years have been the best in a long time—even if I may need plasmapharesis more frequently and there's a good possibility it may not work.

Sometimes when I step into Sloan-Kettering and look around, I still feel frozen, that this can't be my life. It absolutely horrifies me. Every time my middle finger is pricked it's as if it's never happened before. It's routine, but it isn't. Sometimes I finger my neck and can feel the plastic tube in my interior jugular or touch my port and simply can't fathom that this is my life. It just can't be.

But I know it is. And I love it. And I can't say I'd change any of it, even the illness, because it's who I am and without it maybe there wouldn't be Tony Dunne. And that's what it's all about for me. A great part of living with this illness and not losing my sanity involves both looking at the amazing way my life has unfolded after I got sick and accepting I may not get some of the things I want so badly. My health. A baby. A long life. But I did get to be someone I'm proud to be. And I got Tony Dunne.

So I want to be the one beside him as we pull out of the breakfast joint on a Sunday morning. No one but me can know how much I yearn for that, but I think you have a fair idea. But if it can't be me, then I want somebody else to be with him, to love him, to take care of him and in return get all he has to offer. Unlike me, almost all his talents are hidden, which makes the discovery so joyous.

In my mind's eye I often picture Tony on his way home from breakfast, his car climbing the hill and rounding a bend on the back country road. I look to see who is with him.

I can't picture him alone.

Someone has to be in the seat beside him. And as I strain to see, I pray, dear God, how I pray.

Please let it be me.

About the Author

ROSEMARY BRESLIN is a journalist and screenwriter. She has worked at *The New York Times*, *Newsday*, and the New York *Daily News*. Her articles have appeared in *Elle*, *New York* magazine, *Rolling Stone*, and *The New Republic*. She and her husband, Tony Dunne, live in Manhattan.

Printed in the United States
19419LVS00002B/232-234